Project/Infrastructure Finance

Project/Infrastructure Finance

S.K. Bagchi

Professor (Banking and Finance)

NMIMS University, Mumbai

Ane Books Pvt. Ltd.

New Delhi ♦ Chennai

Project/Infrastructure Finance
S.K. Bagchi

Price: Rs. 695/-
Pages: xiv+160= 174 (HB)
Size : Demy (5½" × 8½")
Paper Quality (GSM) : 70

Published by .

Ane Books Pvt. Ltd.

4821, Parwana Bhawan, 1st Floor, 24 Ansari Road, Darya Ganj,
New Delhi - 110 002, Tel.: +91(011) 23276843-44, Fax: +91(011) 23276863
e-mail: kapoor@anebooks.com, Website: www.anebooks.com

Branches

- Avantika Niwas, 1st Floor, 19 Doraiswamy Road, T. Nagar,
  Chennai - 600 017, Tel.: +91(044) 28141554, 28141209
  e-mail: anebookschennai@gmail.com, rathinam@anebooks.com

ISBN : 978-93-8015-646-0

Printed at : R.K. Offset Process, New Delhi.

Dedication

Seeking Heavenly Blessings

from

Father: Late Subhransu Kumar Bagchi

(Passed away on 18-12-1988)

&

Mother: Late Binapani Bagchi

(Passed away on 16-05-2007)

You had first affectionately taught me how to speak, read and write my efforts since then are on, the way both of you desired!

Preface

Project Finance (including infrastructure finance) mechanism has been in operation in the countries as an important facilitator towards industrialisation and/or creation of needed infrastructure comforts in the respective economies.

Infrastructure development process over last two decades has occupied a place of pride and thrust area in almost all the countries of the world in their efforts of providing a full range of welfare amenities to the masses for free or at a deep discount/subsidized tariff and charges. But a major handicap in the process has been identifying sources and raising need-based funds to take care of the massive cost of such projects as are generally the case.

In order to incentivise the Private promoters of repute to increasingly participate in infrastructure projects the Commercial Banks either of their own or in business association with Development Banks/Financial Institutions are motivated to finance liberally, but, within the canons of lending, and, most importantly, within the regulatory setting. The underlying objective, of necessity, is to bring down the funding gap which the Private Promoters and/or state (in case of Public Private Partnership Projects) face generally. Also Medium/Large Industrial Units requiring Project Funding from Banks/ Financial Institutions need to be appropriately supported for the wellbeing of an economy.

With my humble hands-on experience as a Credit Processing Officer for industrial/manufacturing projects in the beginning and, later on as a sanctioning authority in an International Bank for long and thereafter being involved in teaching banking/finance for the budding professionals, I have structured entire aspects of infrastructure financing (including Project Financing) in the form of a hand book now being presented for use by the students undergoing on Projects/Infrastructure Finance, Professional Examination Oriented Courses, the Promoters of such Projects as well as Loan Processing officials at Banks and other Professionals.

In fine, I would respectfully look for suggestions from the users for enriching the contents.

S.K. BAGCHI

Acknowledgement

BANK OF BARODA: The great institution in my life, has shaped me up, polished and then packaged encouragingly over a period of nearly four decades in the area of banking and finance. BOB will forever remain placed on the top of my Head.

My Second innings has by the Grace of God been in an internationally accredited Management Institution – **NMIMS University** (formerly Narsee Monjee Institute of Management), Mumbai. I do respect the care, attention and encouragement and, above all, a unique learning environment here to pursue my teaching and research related endeavours.

I thank the Management, Faculty Members and the Staff of our esteemed institution, in particular, Dr. Sunder Ram Korivi and Dr. Chandan Dasgupta.

Mr. Kumar K.S. Iyer has rendered excellent secretarial services taking all the pressures and pains.

Mr. D.G. Mahabal – basically an Engineer, but later on qualified in Banking and Finance as well creditably, is now recognised as an expert on Project Finance/Infrastructure Finance. He has been kind enough to guide me especially in the preparation of Case Studies. I was fortunate in having an opportunity to work with him for a couple of years during my previous stint in BOB.

My daughter, Saoli, qualified as B.Tech (Mechanical), PGDM, MBA (Finance) and AICWA (Inter) has offered a few valid suggestions in respect of the Contents of the book. Swati, my wife, with her lone involvement in domestic chores and for the wellbeing of the family did the onerous job of assisting me in the editing of the entire manuscript.

Contents

** Wherever in this Book use of the word of Infrastructure Finance only is made, the same may be construed to include generally any industrial financing by way of Project Finance (as mentioned in Chapter No.1 there is very little difference between Project Finance and Infrastructure Finance.)

CHAPTER

1 Understanding Project-Finance

The term 'Project-Finance' is very widely used in the contemporary world of Finance. It occupies Centre Stage in the industrialization process of an economy especially when a country undergoes a transformation/shifting mode from predominantly agrarian stage to a balanced stage of agriculture and industry. For this to happen, the fundamental and basic pre-requisite is the availability of need based financial package – institutional debt component, in particular. Hence, let us look to the various facets of Project-Finance.

DEFINITION OF PROJECT AND FINANCE

The term 'Project' means any planned activity, *e.g.*, starting industry, trade or a small/medium business or writing a Thesis on any subject or any sort of research or other activity. However, in the context of business situation the concept is restricted to any industrial, manufacturing, services activity only (in exclusion of Wholesale/Retail trade or Commercial activity) and often is christened as "Investment Project." Finance ordinarily means loan or money in cash form. Here again the concept is broader to include also, 'non-cash' means of support such as Deferred Payment Bank Guarantee (for acquisition of Capital assets), Other Guarantees/ Letter of Credit etc. Thus, both funded and non-funded sources are clubbed in the financial methodology of 'Finance'.

When we join both the terms Project and Finance, we derive the combined meaning of Project-Finance. In this context, **New Oxford Business Dictionary** states as under:

"Project-Finance is the process of providing money for larger project where the payment of debt will come from Project's Cash Flow". (Here the words money/debt to be understood as both Funded and Non-funded sources as mentioned above).

From practical borrowing/lending aspects, **Prof. J.D. Finnerty** in his book "Project-Financing" states that Project. Financing is "the raising of funds to finance an economically separable capital investment project in which the providers of fund (to include both funded and non-funded as mentioned above) look primarily to the Cash Flow from the project as the source of funds to service the loan".

It will appear from the above discussion that Project-Finance covers:

- Means of finance in the form of Loans/Guarantees/LC for acquisition of fixed assets such as land/building, machinery/equipments and for working capital for 'large' project.
- Repayment to be ensured from the project cash flows. The project assets under finance is to be the security for the financing.

INTER-RELATIONSHIP OF PROJECT-FINANCING AND INFRASTRUCTURE FINANCING

Project-Finance is intended for large sized industrial/allied activities with/without a long gestation period and as such not for any Trading/Commercial activity even if it involves acquisition of land/building (Warehouse for storage of tradeable goods) or any other capital asset. Infrastructure Projects (*i.e.* Power Plant, Construction of Road/Highway etc.) are definitely large projects and involve a wide range of activities till completion, and in the process require high dose of external funded/non-funded form financial support. Depending on the size of project, gestation period is arrived at for the purpose of correlating with repayment programme from the loan/financial support.

Therefore, it is obvious that concept of Project-Financing/Infrastructure financing is very closely inter-linked. In this connection **Prof. Megginson** *et al* have this to state in their Book "*Principles of Corporate Finance*":

"Project Finance Loans (PF) are limited/non-recourse lending to Standalone Companies and they are typically arranged for INFRA-STRUCTURE PROJECTS".

Limited/Non-recourse lending means that the external financial support is backed only by the assets and cash flow of the project – the sponsors of the project do not guarantee payment of loans. However, in Indian pattern of financing, personal/corporate guarantee of promoters is usually stipulated for any Project/Infrastructure Finance Limited.

Clearly, therefore, Project-Financing and Infrastructure Financing is practically one or same mode financing.

BASIC FEATURES OF PROJECT-FINANCE

- It involves starting up a large-sized industrial operation (say Project cost over Rs. 5 crore) or substantial expansion (*i.e.*, increase in business (by over 25 %*) of existing industrial activity by creating a distinct entity SPV or without creating SPV.

- It is generally extended to corporate entities and in some cases to highly rated other structures.
- As against financing an usual project (for acquisition of capital assets etc.) based on viability study of product, Cash flow estimation for long but specific period generally over 5 years is accorded high priority besides viability studies.
- Project financing by a lender encompasses overseeing total financing cycle such as tying up the funded/non-funded (*i.e.*, financial closure) assessed amount, documentation and post-disbursement monitoring activities.
- Sole-lender Project financing is rarely observed. For sharing of Credit risk and sometimes to comply with Prudential lending limits for Single Borrower/Group Borrower the lenders join together and finance the project either on consortium arrangement or on syndication arrangement.
- Project finance is invariably on 'secured' basis (*i.e.*, lender/s having charged by way of Hypothecation/Mortgage on Project assess) especially for Fixed Assets/Current Assets in the Indian Financial System.
- Banks/Financial institutions in India generally finance upto a maximum of 75% of Project Cost.

COMPONENTS OF PROJECT-FINANCE

Any industrial/manufacturing/services investment project would have structured items of initial expenditure before the Project is ready for trial production/trial-run of services. Cost of each item would give rise to total Project Outlay/Total Project Cost. Though each Project has its own features and, in consequence, complexion of items and cost implications, generally in Project-Finance cases following components exist:

- Cost of Land and Construction cost of factory/premises.
- Cost of Plant and Machinery equipments, accessories etc.
- Technical know fees to foreign/domestic technocrats/specialists.
- Support fixed assets such as Furniture, Fire fighting arrangements, vehicles etc.

* Alternatively, it may clearly be defined in terms of Total Project Cost Outlay amount exceeding say 40% of the net worth of the entity (indicative of Risk taking capacity in case the project fails and required to be written off at a later date).

- Pre-operative expenses such as cost of legal services, interest on borrowings till the project starts Commercial production/Services.
- Contingencies (*i.e.*, probable increase in prices of assets required for the period during project construction stage).
- Margin Money for working capital (generally maximum 75% of assessed requirement is financed leaving 25% margin money to be arranged by the promoters).

Since each project has its own specific requirements, the aforesaid components may not universally apply and hence may require to be readjusted on project-specific basis.

SOURCES OF PROJECT-FINANCE

Funding (actual Cash outgo) part of the entire project needs to be appropriately (and conservatively, too) worked out by the Promoters in order that Project does not face any liquidity crisis, especially, during the Construction period. Usual funding pattern is as under:

- Issuance of Equity shares/Preference shares on Private Placement basis initially and at a later stage opening up to public, if necessary, and permissible under regulatory guidelines.
- Issuance of Secured/Unsecured Debentures being debt financing. Convertible Debentures (convertible to Equity shares) when issued take the features of debt-equity financing.
- Secured Term Loan from Banks/Financial Institutions.
- Working Capital finance from Banks.
- Deferred Payment Guarantee from Banks favouring suppliers of Plant and Machinery, fixed assets on specific Credit terms.
- Leasing/Hire Purchase: Obtaining Plant and Machinery Other fixed assets on Lease basis without the requirement of instant Cash funding.
- Unsecured Loan/Deposits from Promoters/Group on market-driven terms and conditions.
- Venture capital finance – depending upon the case.
- Govt. Subsidy/Grants (this may arise especially if the Project is in ***backward*** area).

(For further reading on the aforesaid issue, please refer to the caption "Financial Perspective" in the Chapter 6 on Techniques of Infrastructure Lending).

PROJECT EVALUATION METHODS

The fundamental objective of taking up an investment project is to provide appropriate return to Investors/Stakeholders/Promoters/Investors besides ensuring long term safety of their funds. The external lenders, of course, would be equally interested and as such any project howsoever may be attractive to any enthusiastic investor, must also conform to lending standards upon due diligent study by the lenders.

An evaluation of Project from financial angle is undertaken by any one of the following TWO methods or a combination of both the methods:

1. Discounted Cash Flow Methods (Time value of money concept)
   - Net Present Value (NPV)
   - Internal Rate of Return (IRR)
   - Benefit Cost Ratio (BCR)
2. Non-discounted Cash Flow Methods
   - Accounting Rate of Return (ARR)
   - Pay Back Period (PBP)

Let us look to the above methods in detail.

Under Discounted Cash Flow Method, the future periodical Net Cash flows from the project are discounted (with an assumed discounting factor, say 10%) to arrive at their present values. This process takes the form of Net Present Value (NPV) method and Internal Rate of Return (IRR) method.

(*a*) Net Present Value (NPV):

The Promoters/Lenders may, after a comprehensive analysis of a variety of technical as well as macro and micro economic factors touching the project by Engineers, Economist, Market Research Analysis etc work out a required rate of return. NPV is then arrived at

(*i*) by discounting (*i.e.*, reducing) the future periodical cash flows at the required rate of return (say 10%) and thereafter

(*ii*) out of values so arrived at, to deduct cash outgo for the project (say Rs. 5 crore). After this exercise Project's Positive Cash flow (*i.e.*, NPV being greater than cash outlay of the project) and Negative Cash flow (NPV being lower than Cash outlay) will be found out. If this results in Positive cashflow the project could be considered financially viable – otherwise not.

PRACTICAL APPLICATION

Bhagwan Bhorasha Ltd (BBL) desires to put up a Chemical Plant with an investment of Rs.9000/- (Rs. in crore). The major assumptions are:

- Required rate of return : 10%
- Expected Net Cash Flows.

Rs. in Crores		
First year	:	Rs.5090/-
Second year	:	Rs.4500/-
Third year	:	Rs.4000/-

NPV of the Project will be as under:

Year	Net Cash Flow (Rs. in crore)	Present Value Discount at (PVDF) (10%)	Present Value factor (Rs. in crore)
Initial Cash Outlay (*i.e.*, Zero year)	9000 (–)	—	9000 (–)
First Year return	5090 (+)	0.909.9 *	4627(+) 0.90909 × 5090
Second Year return	4500 (+)	0.826.45 **	3719(+) 0.82645 × 4500
Third Year return	4000 (+)	0.751.31 ***	3005(+) 75131 × 4000

* 1

1.1

** (1)?

1.1

*** 1

(1.1)?

Therefore, Project's estimated position is as under:

Total Cash-in-flows = (4627 + 3719 + 3005) = 11351

Total Cash Outlay = 11351 – 9000 = 2351(+)

Hence, as the Project would have positive Cash flows (- Cash in flows being greater than cash outgo) this would be acceptable.

(Above example has been placed with suitable additions / modifications from the base example provided by Prof. Graham Peirson *et al* in their book '*Business Finance*').

(*b*) Initial Rate of Return (IRR):

Under IRR unlike the concept of Positive Cash flow as the benchmark, the rate of return of future Cash flows are equal to initial Cash outlay, will determine financial viability IRR method takes into account:

Discount factor (as in NPV) + Highest rate of interest the promoters/investors would be prepared to pay assuming almost entire portion project is based in borrowed fund (Borrowed funds to be serviced out of periodical Cash-in-flows of the project).

If IRR of Future Cash Flows (say of First Year, Second Year and Third Year equals to initial cash outlay of Rs.9000 (crore) as per above example under NPV works out 25% on the basis of future cash flows being equal to Rs. 9000 (crore) by trial and error method and if the required rate of return of Promoter's/Investors is 15%, the Project would obviously be acceptable.

Alternate Definition of IRR: It is that rate of discounting applied on future cash flows to be generated by the project which makes the sum of all future cash flows equal to the present value of total investment made into the project.

(*c*) Benefit Cost Ratio (BCR):

Numerator = Present value of total year wise cash-in-flows from the Project

Denominator = Initial Investment (Cost)

The example of BCR computation is as under:-

Numerator = 4627 + 3719 + 3005 = 11351

Denominator = 9000

BCR = 1.261 Criteria is if BCR > 1 Accept the Project.

(*d*) Accounting Rate of Return (ARR):

For financial assessment of a Project under ARR the following aspects are considered:

(*i*) Yearwise net Profit (after taking into account Depreciation on Project Assets and Income Tax etc).

(*ii*) Initial Project Outlay is compared with average annual earnings.

(*iii*) Average annual Net Profit (after depreciation and Income Tax) receipts divided by Project Outlay.

(*iv*) Thereafter, required rate of return (as may be expected by the Promoters/Investors) is compared with ARR.

(*v*) If ARR is greater than required rate of return, the project is acceptable.

(*e*) Pay Back Period (PBP):

Under PBP the following aspects are considered:

- Initial Cash outlay of the Project is decided.
- Project should be such that above cash outlay is recovered from net cash flows by summing up the flows year-after-year till the aggregate amount is equal to initial cash outlay.
- Maximum acceptable Payback period is fixed by the Promoters/ Investors.
- Where PPP is shorter than maximum period set to the project would be acceptable.

FINAL COMMENTS ON PROJECT EVALUATION METHODS

Discounted Cash Flow method as compared with Non-discounted Cash Flow method is widely practiced in assessing financial viability of large projects with fairly long gestation period and dependent substantially on borrowed funds. However, often discounted method is compared with the outcome of any non-discounted method for financial evaluation in the context of the risk philosophy and risk appetite of the Promoters/Investors.

Of the two Discounted methods (NPV and IRR), NPV is usually more suited to large sectors primarily because of its consistent outcome. Quoted below is the expert comments from Prof. Graham Peirson *et al* from their book '*Business Finance*':

"We recommend the net present value method because it is consistent with the objective of maximizing shareholders' wealth. It is simple to use and gives rise to fewer problems than Internal Rate of Return Method".

It was observed generally that investors/lenders preferred NPV methods as against IRR method as per the survey undertaken in Australia a four years ago.

PROJECT RISK ANALYSIS

It is now an internationally settled view that a project to be acceptable to the stakeholders must successfully pass through techno-economic viability including Project return evaluation. Alongside this as a matter of safe commercial practice the project estimates are pressed into a Stress Testing Module (also known as Sensitivity Analysis, Scenario Analysis). Under Stress Testing Method main Project Income (*i.e.*, Sales, etc) as estimated is subjected to discounted factor (say 5%, 10% etc.) as may be considered appropriate on case to cash basis. Thereafter, the resultant reduced Income level is refocussed and examined with respect to debt-repayment capacity/

Investor return expectations. If arising out of the exercise the project is expected to be on its feet by all means, it may be considered that the Project is adoptable from such risk angle of adverse movements of expected main Income.

PROJECT COMPLETION AUDIT

During the project construction stage the lenders, in particular, (besides other Investors) overview the progress and compare the same with the accepted plan. Any deviation is taken up for remedial action.

In addition to the above it is necessary to put in place a structured arrangement by way of Post Completion Control Audit. However, the word 'Audit' is hot intended to mean any statutory mandate but, in fact, an assessment of the Project's overall features when completed in all respects. Such a study is quite relevant and important, too, from the view point of major lenders/investors stake in the project. The study should cover:

- Whether any major deviation has taken place in the matter of cash outflows as compared to the budgeted amount.
- Whether any specific measures are to be considered to ensure project's operating performance especially when the cash outflow had significant variation.
- Such a system puts a sort of performance checks of this promoters as to the quality of their investment decisions and smooth execution.
- Some part of project activity as originally planned may have to be relooked in light of any macro/micro developments in the interim period and as such where necessary may even be done away with to ensure the project's well-being.

The Project Completion Audit to be undertaken only once from the angle of lenders/investors should be carried out by highly experienced Project Experts who may be their in-house personnel or External Specialists.

❑❑❑

CHAPTER

2 Infrastructure Anatomy

The term 'Infrastructure' now so dear and near to all of us, is derived from Latin word ***Infrastructura* ('a' in place of 'e')** meaning broadly a platform / environment below/within which the facilities or means of comforts exist for day to day living of people/growth or prosperity of organisations – in short "Structural Foundations". In that context, all physical and social components of comforts / necessaries fall within the ambit of the term which is christened as SOCIAL OVERHEAD CAPITAL by World Bank. A renewed focus is being noticed in most of the countries especially, in emerging ones like India, China etc., for all-round infrastructural development since the beginning of 1980s.

INFRASTRUCTURE DEFINED

There is no statutory definition of Infrastructure applicable in all cases/ situations. Presented below a few accredited definitions:

According to **World Bank**, "*Infrastructure is an integral part of development providing and delivering basic services that people need for every day life e.g., safe drinking water, electricity, roads, sanitation etc.*"

According to **India Infrastructure Report** (Rakesh Mohan Committee) – Economic approach:

"*Infrastructure is generally defined as the physical framework of facilities through which goods and services are provided to the public. It's linkages to the economy are multiple and complex, because it affects production and consumption directly, creates negative and positive spillover effects (externalities) and involves large flow of expenditure.*"

Prof. John Jackson *et al.* have provided a further illustrative economic definition as under:

"*Infrastructure comprises ample water, waste treatment transport, training, research, financial institutions, management, Public Relations Consultants and so on. A rich infrastructure can be one of the strongest agglomerative forces explaining the continuing growth.*"

RESERVE BANK OF INDIA

RBI has provided a composite definition of Infrastructure lending not simply on infrastructure alone. As per **RBI** "any credit facility in whatever form extended by lenders, banks, Financial Institutions (FIs) or Non-banking Finance Companies (NBFCs) to an infrastructure facility as stated below falls within the definition of 'Infrastructure lending'. In other words, a credit facility provided to a borrower engaged in:

- Developing, or
- Operating and maintaining, or
- Developing, operating and maintaining any infrastructure facility that is a project in any of the following sectors, or any infrastructure facility of a similar nature:

  (*i*) a road, including toll road, a bridge or a rail system;

  (*ii*) a highway project including other activities being an integral part of the highway project;

  (*iii*) a port, airport, inland waterway or inland port;

  (*iv*) a water supply project, irrigation project, water treatment system, sanitation and sewerage system or solid waste management system;

  (*v*) telecommunication services whether basic or cellular, including radio paging, domestic satellite service (*i.e.*, a satellite owned and operated by an Indian company for providing telecommunication service), network of trunking, broadband network and internet services;

  (*vi*) an industrial park or *special economic zone*;

  (*vii*) generation or generation and distribution of power;

  (*viii*) transmission or distribution of power by laying a network of new transmission or distribution lines;

  (*ix*) construction relating to projects involving agro-processing and supply of inputs to agriculture;

  (*x*) construction for preservation and storage of processed agro-products, perishable goods such as fruits, vegetables and flowers including testing facilities for quality;

  (*xi*) construction of educational institutions and hospitals;

  (*xii*) any other infrastructure facility of similar nature.

In view of the aforesaid varieties of definitions one should be guided by the approach to any issue on infrastructure, while looking to its various facets rather than adopting a particular mode of definition from lending angle. However, RBI definition as above is of mandatory nature in India from lending perspective.

TYPES OF INFRASTRUCTURE

Broadly, Infrastructure may be classified under two groups:

(*A*) Physical Infrastructure which generally covers the following:

(*i*) Transportation including urban mass transportation: Roadways, Railways, Airways and water supply and transportation etc.
(*ii*) Power Generation, transmission and distribution.
(*iii*) Telecommunications
(*iv*) Port handling facilities
(*v*) Solid waste collection and disposal facilities
(*vi*) Irrigation facilities

Special Economic Zone (SEZ) has a different characteristic in as much as it contains all the ingredients of a physical infrastructure while being otherwise considerably led by "Real Estate Intervention".

(*B*) Social Infrastructure generally covers the following:

(*i*) Education (Secondary and above)
(*ii*) Primary Mass Education Facilities
(*iii*) Medical – (Health)
(*iv*) Sanitation and Sewerage
(*v*) Legal and General administrative framework

DISTINCTION BETWEEN PHYSICAL INFRASTRUCTURE AND SOCIAL INFRASTRUCTURE

Physical Infrastructure	Social Infrastructure
1. This sector directly assists in enhancing, maintaining productive capacity of a country.	**1.** This sector contributes indirectly since its components have hardly any direct role in productive sectors.
2. This is capital intensive as putting up/enhancing this sector requires huge Capital expenditure in some cases *i.e.* port, power irrigation, transportation etc.	**2.** Generally the issue of any major capital expenditure does not arise.
3. Public Private Partnership model may suit the sector.	**3.** Public Private Partnership model has a very limited role – in some cases may not arise at all *e.g.*, Legal and administrative framework.
4. Facilities under this sector are generally provided on cost recoupment basis – the users should pay something for the services.	**4.** Facilities under this group are generally 'free' or at a very low pricing basis *i.e.*, Treatment in Government Hospital Public Sanitation Facilities etc.

Physical Infrastructure	Social Infrastructure
5. 'Gestation Period' for the outcome of such facilities sometimes may be long *e.g.*, Irrigation, Port handling facilities etc.	**5.** Very low time span is generally involved for implementation of any project under this sector.

SCOPE AND IMPORTANCE OF INFRASTRUCTURE DEVELOPMENT

Infrastructure applies 'grease' to the productive sectors and also uniquely provides a framework for poverty reduction, and safe and smooth of human living in this planet of ours.

SCOPE

Infrastructure services give rise to intermediate inputs to the productive sectors and thus often referred to as "unpaid factor of production" since it's availability leads to higher obtainable from other capital and labour". (Article on Infrastructure development by Mr. G. Raghuram.) Infrastructure sector covers a heterogeneous group of services/facilities in physical and social areas (as mentioned above) which obviously are common in all the countries. However, the relative higher focus on a particular sector *e.g.*, Power generator etc. is dependent upon a country's overall social, political and economic environment and the overall perception of the people of the country. Thus, with the broad framework of 'Infrastructure' the scope of attainment may vary from country to country.

The entire aspect of contribution of infrastructure sector may be viewed from the following aspects:

1. Infrastructure is the conduit pipe for economic capital and core promotional activity such as power, water and roads.
2. Infrastructure is a strong mover of activity *e.g.*, railway services provide useful services for carrying goods from the supplier to markets.
3. Welfare facilities such as Primary Schools, Hospitals etc. serve mass requirements at low/no cost especially when under state funding.
4. Infrastructure projects being capital intensive *e.g.*, construction of water storage dam or electrical generating plant etc., State funding may often need to be supplemented by private funding.

IMPORTANCE OF INFRASTRUCTURE

The existence of an appropriate level of Infrastructure stock ensures safe, smooth, healthy development of productive sectors and overall human development index of a country. But mere thrust on a wide range of infrastructure amenities is not enough and must be supported by necessary financial, administrative and legal framework to provide the expected outcome. World Bank has observed that greater focus needs to be placed on QUALITY NOT QUANTITY of Infrastructure services.

Infrastructure sector is important mainly from the following perspectives:

(*i*) as a key driver for all-round growth with enhancement in the efficiency level.

(*ii*) most infrastructure utilities *e.g.*, Education, Supply of Clean Drinking Water, Health, Sanitation etc. touch the population at all levels.

(*iii*) upkeeping of environment for safe living.

(*iv*) poverty alleviation as a consequence of overall development of productive sectors.

(*v*) easy and cost-efficient access to international markets both for inputs and outputs is possible out of infrastructure developments.

It may be appropriate here to quote relevant portion from India Infrastructure Report on the importance of infrastructure sector in our country:

"The availability of adequate infrastructure is imperative for the overall economic development of the country. Infrastructure adequacy helps determine success in diversifying production, expanding trade, coping with population growth, reducing poverty and improving environmental conditions".

BASIC BOTTLENECKS

Infrastructural development is essentially a state-level responsibility – often, however, performed in association with and on co-operation from Non-Governmental social agencies of developments when available in a country. Poor infrastructure is a social parasite and poses all the bottlenecks in an healthy creation and maintenance of an infrastructural platform. The usual bottlenecks are:

(*i*) Bureaucratic style of managing infrastructure sector with attendant red-tapism and unhealthy work culture – this is more pronounced in a democratic form of Government structure.

(*ii*) Inefficiency and waste in planning investment, and regulation of infrastructure services thereby losing opportunities of poverty reduction and environmental upgradation.

(*iii*) Infrastructure development generally involves huge capital expenditure not always matching with budgetary source finance.

(*iv*) Inadequate attention to population growth and urbanization.

(*v*) Poor maintenance of infrastructure facilities already created.

(*vi*) Ineffective/Inadequate use of contemporary technologies to broaden infrastructural facilities.

(*vii*) Amongst the infrastructural development agencies (Private Sectors) nurturing a feeling of "Competition for others and monopoly for self" affects infrastructural development.

SOLUTIONS

In order to overcome the bottlenecks in infrastructural developments following aspects need to be looked into keeping in view the views of World Bank and other authorities:

(*i*) Eradication of poverty through concerned efforts of accelerations physical and social infrastructure.

(*ii*) Universal Primary education, gender equality and empowerment.

(*iii*) Move to ensure environmental sustainability by taking steps to remedy the deficiencies instantly.

(*iv*) Encouraging joint action plan of infrastructure development through 'Public Private Partnership' (PPP) and incentivise competition in various PPP projects, providing tax concessions etc.

(*v*) Fast track clearance of infrastructural projects by fixing a realistic time-band of approval, funding and infrastructure.

In short, removal of bottlenecks depends on the degree of concerns of the Government as also active involvement of all the players in the market economy. The World Bank has this to say.

"Coping with infrastructure's future challenge involves much more than a simple numbers game of drawing up inventories of infrastructure stocks and plotting needed investments on the basis of past patterns. It involves tackling inefficiency and waste ...."

WORLD SCENARIO

The World Bank is better placed to examine the outcome of infrastructural development aspects in the countries. In this respect, they have observed, *inter alia*:

- Developing Countries generally invest around USD 200 bn annually.
- 80% of national output and 20% of their overall investment are made available for infrastructure sector.

- While improving signs are noticed in the area of
  - (*i*) Transport, power, water and sanitation services
  - (*ii*) Provision of clean water
  - (*iii*) Telephone connections etc., they are not considered sufficient in view of:
    - (*a*) Nearly 200 crore of People (out of World Population of about 600 crore) lack adequate sanitation.
    - (*b*) Similarly electric power has yet to reach nearly 200 crore of people.
    - (*c*) Demand for modern productive facilities and avenues for international competitiveness far outstrip existing capacity.

INFRASTRUCTURE GAP IN INDIA

As per Press Report the Infrastructure Gap in India in Electric Power, Rail and Airport sectors as against USA, UK, China is huge. This is evident from the following:

INITIATIVES IN INDIA

PARTICULARS	INDIA	US	UK	CHINA
Electric Consumption per Capita (kWH)	618	14,240	6,756	1,684
Roads per Million People (km)	2,983	21,443	6,467	1,471
Rail Route per Million People (km)	56	755	276	57
Cargo Handled at Ports per Capita (kg)	572	7,953	9,733	4,265
No. of Passengers Handled at Airports per 1,000 Persons	71	4,780	3,517	151

In the "Infrastructure Review", the Infrastructure Development Finance Ltd., has succinctly put as under the initiative being shown in the area of infrastructural development.

"Realising the significance of infrastructure, the Government (Government of India) has been shown increasing commitment to ensure growth and sustainable delivery of infrastructure services at low prices".

It has since been reported in the press that Government of India may ensure investment in Infrastructure projects over next five years of around USD 500 bn (approx as 20 lac crore.

The position in some major infrastructural sectors may be summarised as follows:

Power: Government of India has taken measures to provide for development of large-sized Ultra Mega Power Projects at Coal Pitheads and Costal locations. Provision has been made for investment of Rs.9 lac crore for supply of power to all under the mission "power for all" by the year 2012.

Telecom: Besides substantially reducing telephone charges especially STD Call charges, the move has been taken to effect suitable changes in Access Deficit charges and license fees. Broad Policy for accelerating the growth of internet services has also been put in place. It is reported that *Tele-Density* (*i.e.*, number of Telephones per 100 persons) now stands at 22.52 compared to 2.8 in the year 1999.

Transportation: In Civil Aviation Sector, open Sky Policy as also other allied measures is proving desired outcome to the people besides revenue increase for the Government. Railways have been taking various passenger-friendly measures on an ongoing basis. Modernisation plans such as Freight corridor and Metro Railway would accelerate transportation facilities in the country.

Road Development (Highway/Expressway): National Highway Development Project (Golden Quadrilateral) is being implemented in partnership with private sector in phases and favourable outcome is in sight. To finance smoothly the massive expenditure involved in Highway/Expressway Construction, 100% Foreign Direct Investment (FDI) is allowed.

Ports and Shipping: A policy for Maritime Sector (Port, Shipping and Inland transport) has been conceptualized on the principle that Government should be concerned only with policy making, resource generation and regulation leaving day-to-day administration to identified units/organisations. This is expected to boost up these areas of infrastructural utility.

In addition to the aforesaid initiatives, the other areas being activated are as under:

Urban Infrastructure: Jawaharlal Nehru Urban Renewal Mission has been launched to accelerate urban services, particularly, development of small and medium towns.

Commercial Infrastructure: The location of various Special Economic Zone (SEZs) is expected to come up as a major source for overall progress of the country when the current debate about the desirability of such as initiative is finally set at rest.

In regard to the initiatives of Government of India, a recent press report *inter alia*, provides as under:

VISIBLE GROWTH

Planning Commission Consultation paper of Oct. 2007 shows visible growth with various Infrastructure sectors as under:

INFRASTRUCTURE-VISIBLE GROWTH ACROSS SECTORS

Sectors	Xth Plan (Anti.Inv.) 02-07		XIth Plan (Anti-Inv.) 07-12		Remarks
	US ($ bn)	Sectoral Share (%)	US ($ bn)	Sectoral Share (%)	
Power	75	33	158	30	Momentum to accelerate, spread to transmission and distribution
Roads and Bridges	37	16	80	15	Continuing momentum
Telecommunication	32	14	68	13	Continuing momentum
Railways	31	14	66	13	Dark horse-improved profitability will lead to higher investments
Irrigation	29	13	57	11	Focus Area
Ports	1	0.5	19	4	Renewed focus
Airports	2	0.8	9	2	Renewed focus – could see higher investments than planned
Others	20	9	62	12	Urban Infrastructure – a new focus area
Total	227	100	519	100	

"A number of initiatives have been taken in streamlining contract award procedures, formulating model concession agreements, building viability gap funding windows and finalizing a panel of advisors to structure projects for the private sector...."

PUBLIC PRIVATE PARTNERSHIP

The Government has decided as a major policy stance that in order to effect desired cost saving and to facilitate access to expertise and proprietary technology and to provide supplementary source of finance towards multi-faceted infrastructure development at a faster rate, Public Private Purchasing model be adopted on case to case basis.

Private equity subscription is expected to be minimum 15% under this model as has recently been decided in case of 50,000 kms road projects every next 10 years.

WHAT IS EXACTLY PUBLIC PRIVATE PARTNERSHIP (PPP) IN INFRASTRUCTURE?

There is no standard definition of PPP in any country. In a very simple and obvious manner PPP may be defined as a co-operative venture between Public (*i.e.*, Govt) and Private Sectors. As a matter of fact, PPP covers following main aspects:

— it is a long term Contractual Partnership (25 years +) between Government and Private sectors (mainly Corporates).

— such Partnership to cover infrastructural sectors which are traditionally within the sole ambit of Public Sector (Construction of roads etc).

— the partnership usually covers:

- financing
- designing
- implementing
- operating

In short, Public Sector Capital Contribution gives rise to:

— Sovereign responsibilities

— Public accountability

On the other hand, Private Sector Capital funding provides:

— Private sector higher order efficiency level

— Business incentives on a sustainable manner

WHY PRIVATE SECTORS ARE INTERESTED?

- Scope for reasonable return on opportunities arising out of funding gap of investment which Government may not be in a position to meet out of fiscal resources.
- Tax Concessions usually allowed by democratic form of Governments to foster infrastructure development.
- To participate in market competition in areas which were monopolised by Government.
- To evolve Contemporary environmentally-friendly projects christened as 'Greenfield Projects' and implement the same on Commercial basis.

EMBEDDED OPTION

With a view to ensuring smooth implementation and continuation of infrastructural projects involving Private sector participation a provision of Embedded Option in the contract is often made. Such an option serves the following aspects:

- Government's option to legislate or contract to provide Guarantees.
- Such guarantees may cover:
  (*a*) minimum revenue stream
  (*b*) anti-competition adventures
  (*c*) restriction of pricing of services for a specific period.

An assessment of outcome of PPP model in India shows that while it is quite successful in case of sectors like

(*i*) telecom
(*ii*) Power
(*iii*) Roads and
(*iv*) Ports, it is not so in the areas of education and health. The underlying reasons are that people do not like private intervention in education and health for fear of exploitive tariff/charges.

SOME MYTHS ABOUT INFRASTRUCTURE DEVELOPMENT

There are a few widely believed wrong notions in the infrastructure development process especially in a democratic form of Government administration which are mentioned below:

MYTH NO. 1: It is believed that Government should undertake full duty and responsibility in the infrastructure development of a country.

While it is true that any Government worth the name and form should concern itself substantially in the infrastructure matters, it is also reasonably expected that every citizen has his/her role in the process, *e.g.*, keeping environment clean and free from pollution. Furthermore, the affluent citizens are also expected to provide funding to the Government, for example, paying due taxes, subscribing to low-yielded Infrastructure Development Bonds issued by the Government from time to time.

MYTH NO. 2: Infrastructure services should always be 'subsidized' by the Government.

True, infrastructure projects touch all state of people – rich, middle income earner poor and below poverty line people (*i.e.*, income level of an individual not exceeding USD 1.00 daily *i.e.*, around Rs.40/- daily) and hence must be provided on concessions terms. But it should not be expected as a matter of long-run development of a country that Government should continue to provide subsidies for such sector since such subsidies may mean a burden on a few by way of direct/indirect taxation. Ideally, infrastructure projects should be on: Cost plus a very low level of return so as to preside a proprietary incentive.

MYTH NO. 3: Infrastructure sector should always remain a 'State Monopoly'- and no private participation.

It may be a fact that private investment in any project is triggered more by 'profit motive' and less on social concern. It may also be stated that in the contemporary world scenario a state should not pay whole and sole attention to sectors but should more be engaged in overall 'governance'. Moreover, the resource mobilization on an increasing scale (as is necessary for infrastructure sector) may not be possible by a State alone. Hence, Public Private Partnership model with overall authorities over the Government is now the order of the day in infrastructure development process.

MYTH NO. 4: Any Infrastructure project should be managed in totality and no splitting up of sub activities is advisable.

Any infrastructure activity involves asset location, asset operation, maintenance and asset security. If a particular project is relatively small say, modernization of a particular port, particular power sector or surface road, the managing of entire activity may be reasonably possible. But large-sized power, telecommunication or Highway Projects should preferably be unbundled into 'logical subactivities' especially in asset maintenance and customer service areas so as to provide hassle free and appropriate services on a continuing basis.

MYTH NO. 5: Foreign Capital flows being of a transient nature (as it mostly to reap the benefits of regulatory arbitrage, *i.e.*, interest differentials) should not be invested by the state towards infrastructure development.

It may be fairly right to assume that NRI inflows are not of a permanent nature while investment in infrastructure is of long term dimension. But, it is more true that key constraint to potential growth of productive capacity in an emerging economy, in particular, is relatively low levels of infrastructure investment which again is often caused by inadequate fund flows required for the purpose. Hence, the solution obviously lies with using foreign capital flows limited to a certain level of such flows for infrastructure development. It is reported that Government of India is inclined utilize around 2% of the foreign currency resources towards infrastructure development.

MYTH NO. 6: Infrastructure Projects should be treated at par with any commercial project – hence Income Tax Exemption as is now should be withdrawn.

It is true that some of the infrastructure projects especially, Power, Transport etc. are no different than any Commercial project. It is also equally true that for boosting of investment by Private sectors in various infrastructure projects, incentive by way of income tax relief may need to be continued for some more time. Agricultural Income is also presently exempted from Income Tax. The agricultural operations also are of commercial nature. Should then we withdraw income tax exemption from this sector also at this stage of country's level of growth and property ?

It would appear from all the stated above that at the current stage of world-wide development, infrastructure project has to be viewed with utmost priority and where possible on Public Private Partnership model preferably.

REGULATORY CHALLENGE

The Government of a country is the ultimate REGULATOR in any activity. For the sake of smooth administration various regulatory outfits are created by the Government, *e.g.*, Telecom Regulatory Authority etc. The Government remains responsible and accountable for infrastructure sectors like other sectors, *e.g.*, financial services etc.

In meeting with the expectations of various stakeholders in the society, day-to-day providers of infrastructural inputs/services on one hand, and Revenue Management of the Government by way of taxation, regulatory license fees etc. on the other hand, there are certain areas of CHALLENGE a Government, especially, democratic form of Government has to face on an ongoing basis as under as considered by World Bank:

1. ***Demand from Non-Poor:*** Reduce direct/indirect taxes especially entertainment taxes.

2. ***Demand from those below poverty line:*** To broad coverage of services, *e.g.*, to establish Primary schools at every village, Public Non-fee paying Latrines at villages etc.
3. ***Expectations from Providers of infrastructure inputs/services:*** To secure maximum levels of profits and to enjoy maximum privilege *e.g.*, exemption from Income Tax etc.

Finally, State faces its own challenge as it endeavours to reduce/eliminate subsidies and to earn reasonable return for provision of all types of utility services without focus on the any level income of the people. Arising out of the aforesaid areas, in the context of developing countries, Mr. Ajay Sagar rightly states "…. regulators in developing countries need to pay attention to issues relating to

(*i*) Corporate governance practices,
(*ii*) Adoption of sound accounting and disclosure practice,
(*iii*) Transparency standards,
(*iv*) Corporate social responsibility,
(*v*) Environmental management, and
(*vi*) Development of Capital market infrastructure."

It is, therefore, evident that in a socio-economic pattern of state administration the aforesaid regulatory challenges are often of significant dimension in a country. While it is generally true that Government of India has been managing infrastructure sectors on a priority basis, efforts are needed in several areas. In this context, Mr. S. Murlidharan – a commenter on infrastructure sector, has observed; "The infrastructure regulatory scenario in India has till date, been characterized by a distinct lack of coordination and a focus on short-term goals. This is primarily due to the slow progress of privatization over the last 15 years, concomitant with the fears of replacing a state monopoly with a private monopoly."

REGULATORY CAPTURE

The word 'Capture' in the context of any regulatory framework in infrastructure projects denotes the scope of any sort of control by those regulated (Promoters) upon framing the policy issues by regulatory authorities. The concept of regulatory capture, in general, was developed by Nobel Laureate Economist **Dr. George Stizler**.

The basic concerns revolving the issue are:

— How the vested interests of the promoters reflect on the regulations through political interests – if there be really any, should a regulator be driven more by the interests of the regulated entities than by public interest ?

— Should a regulator forfeit any autonomy/independence even under any severe pools and pressures arising out of political interests?

It is widely acknowledged that Political risks generally carry significant bearing on infrastructural projects. Hence, it must be ensured that there should not be any regulatory capture under any circumstances.

CORPORATE GOVERNANCE ISSUES

Managing an infrastructural sector casts somewhat different approach and of special dimension since fund outlay is huge on the one hand, and return on investment is lesser in proportion as compared to any other economic activity, while there are a lot of reflections on Social Welfare aspects.

Hence, if any infrastructure activity is run on Private initiative or on Public Private Partnership (PPP) model, Corporate Governance issues are to be well cared of on a continuing and self-imposed basis.

Usually, the Corporate Governance in Infrastructure sector may contain the following elements:

- Social well-being to be the primary motto although commercial aspects also to be kept in view.
- Proactive professional approach to be displayed as a rule – any consumer grievance to be resolved on a time bound basis.
- Transparency and Disclosure on all major policy issues especially pricing of services, *e.g.*, Highway Vehicle Movements Toll Tax, Power tariff etc.

In case of PPP projects, Government should have a compact mechanism *to monitor and control* the Private Partner's day-to-day concern and involvement in running the services.

❑❑❑

CHAPTER

3 Finance for Infrastructure

Infrastructure is the foundation of any country. Without the existence of an appropriate level of physical and social infrastructure the people in a country would remain deprived of the vital support in their every day life. But it is also true that creation, utilisation and maintenance of infrastructural services need sustainable financial support since in majority of cases huge capital expenditure is involved in the process. The financing of infrastructure project through state budgetary support has been a traditional window. However, it has already been realized that state alone cannot feed the growing demand of this sector financially. Thus, the issues of alternative sources of resource raising in infrastructure projects assume importance.

WHY INSTITUTIONAL FINANCE NECESSARY?

In the contemporary world of finance, the Institutional Window for finding an infrastructural project is required to be availed of due recently to the following reasons:

(*i*) Financial requirement of an infrastructural project is generally huge which may not always be possible to be met through state budgetary support and/or Private funding.

(*ii*) Commercial viability of an infrastructure sector is dependant upon a host of socio-economic – politico factors. Hence, non-institutional investors may not always feel encouraged to put in their funds for such purposes to the extent necessary.

(*iii*) Institutional funding, especially from Public Sector Financial Institutions (as in India), is cheaper than any other alternative external source of funding.

(*iv*) Income generation time in infrastructure project is generally longer and, hence, longer repayment schedule for Infrastructure finance is necessary which is usually possible from Institutional sources subject, however, to fulfillment of viability criteria.

(*v*) Funding Cost (Interest/service charges) for Institutional borrowing provides for hassle free Income tax permissible deduction item, while cost of owners' fund etc is not so. Again, cost of Non-institute funding may require adequate documentary support/ justification to claim Income tax benefit.

(*vi*) Financial monitoring at Post disbursement stage, especially, end-use verification aspects is necessary on a continuing basis. The Institutional funding mechanism presides for such an arrangement to ensure safety of funds at any point of time.

PROJECT-FINANCE/OBJECT FINANCE APPROACH

Project-Finance implies that funding for any industrial/manufacturing/ servicing/socially beneficial sector involves:

- Huge investment in capital assets/fixed assets.
- Large quantum of Project outlay and funding.
- Long gestation period from the time of project conception till fund generation.
- Long repayment programme (usually 20-25 years +) with initial moratorium of 3-5 years.
- Availability of income generation from non-project sources (*e.g.*, rental income of property let out, if any, surplus income available from other projects etc.)

Object Finance (also known as Non-recourse financing), on the other hand, implies funding of a project with following in view:

- Huge investment in Capital asset/Fixed asset as in case of Project Finance but viewed separately project-wise *e.g.*, funding Power Project in Place '*A*' to be viewed separately from Place '*B*' etc.
- Gestation period may not always be long *e.g.*, financing cost of Aircraft, Ship, Satellite may generate income soon.
- Repayment for funding to be linked project-wise, *i.e.*, Income from Power Project '*A*' should not be utilised for Loan repayment of Project '*B*'. Further non-project income should not be utilised for project repayment.
- Revenue for the project should be derived from the project source only by way of user-fee tolls/other cash flow, escrow mechanisms etc.

DETAILED POINTS OF – DISTINCTION BETWEEN PROJECT FINANCE AND OBJECT FINANCE

Project Finance	Object Finance
1. This mode of finance is available for new as well refinancing old projects.	**1.** This mode of finance is available for new projects only.
2. The lender is to look to the revenues from the particular financed projects and also to the security of project assets.	**2.** The lender is to look predominantly to the revenues from the particularly financed project though financed assets are required to be encumbered to the lender.
3. Projects generally involve large, complex and expensive installations for overall commercial proposes *e.g.*, Steel Industry.	**3.** Generally, immovable capital assets under identified infrastructure sector *e.g.*, Highway, Power plant etc. are considered.
4. The borrower generally may be a special purpose entity.	**4.** The borrower need not necessarily be a special purpose entity although Special Propose Vehicle Mechanism may be formed from lending point of view.
5. The borrower has to operate the project and derive revenues from the same. Rental arrangement of the project is not covered.	**5.** Rental or lease contracts of the financed assets with one or various parties is permissible.
6. Under Risk Management approach of supervisory slotting criteria (-5- supervisory risk weight grades as per Basel Accord), 'asset characteristics' with respect to configuration, size, design and maintenance of security (e.g., age, size of aircraft) is not treated as a parameter.	**6.** 'Asset characteristics' is one of the important supervisory parameters for risk weight grading.

WHAT IS THEN STATUS OF INFRASTRUCTURE PROJECT?

Infrastructural Projects should be treated as Object Finance in light of the above.

TYPES OF INFRASTRUCTURAL FINANCE AVAILABLE FROM BANKS/FINANCIAL INSTITUTIONS

The word, Finance has, over last two decades, passed through a variety of transformation phases beginning originally with short term funding or overdraft type to the present day stature of non-funded assistance. There is hardly any distinction being made in banking business in between extending a funded facility and non-funded facility insofaras risk management attributes are concerned.

In case of infrastructure projects the guidelines issued by RBI permit banks extending the following types of financial assistance:

Fund-based	Non-fund based
1. Term Loan	**1.** Term Bank Guarantee (Deferred Payment Guarantee)
2. Cash Credit	**2.** Short Term Bank Guarantee for procurement of raw materials/inputs, performance Guarantee.
3. Unsecured (Clean) Overdraft	**3.** Short term Bank Guarantee for obtaining unsecured Loan from others.
4. Bills Purchase/Bills Discounting Facilities	**4.** Letter of Credit Facility.

In addition to the above, RBI has accorded special permission in respect of Infrastructural sector for the following:

(*i*) Loan for financing the acquisition of promoter's share in an existing company (where the existing foreign promoters/others voluntarily propose to disinvest). Such Loan should be limited to a maximum of 50% of the requirement. Tenure of the Loan should not normally exceed 7 years.

(*ii*) Finance by way of subscription to Bonds/Debentures/Preference/ Equity shares, although this will be shown as Investment by banks, such finance will be treated as Deemed Advance.

(*iii*) Inter-Institutional Guarantees: A Bank may issue Guarantees to other Lending Institutions provided it takes up at least 5% Project Cost as a funded advance facility.

SALIENT FEATURES OF FINANCING

(*a*) Term Loan component for purchase/acquisition of land/building, Plant and Machinery, Equipments etc has a dominant share on overall funding requirement. Depending upon case to case project outlay term loan requirement may even go upto 75% of Project Cost.

(*b*) Tenure for Term Loan may be of 20-25 years as against normal term Loan of 5-7 years.

(*c*) Working Capital finance for purchase of raw materials/inputs and for meeting day-to-day running expenses may be generally around 5% of Project Cost since mostly such projects are run on cash/ low credit terms.

(*d*) For the balance being Promoters' Contribution/Owned Fund Component, the some may be around 20%.

(*e*) Bills Purchase/Bill Discounting facilities may rarely arise – and, if it does in any case, the same would be within 5% of Working Capital Component as stated (*c*) above.

(*f*) Out of Non-funded facility, Deferred Payment Guarantee/Letter of Credit for Capital Goods generally claim major share and these facilities wherever extended generally within 75% term loan component (*a*) above.

(*g*) In some cases, especially in telecom sector, Performance Gurantee may be required.

(*h*) In projects on Public Private Partnership model Government being Co-obligant, Credit risk is relatively low.

(*i*) Since financial requirements of most of the infrastructure projects are huge running over a few crores of rupees, consortium financial/ syndication form of financing amongst a group of willing lenders is generally the practice as a point of credit risk diffusion and/ or liquidity issue of participating Banks/Financial institutions.

TAKE OUT FINANCING

Infrastructure finance is essentially of a long term nature say 20-25 years during which time resource of financing bank remains blocked. Again a bank's resource base is predominantly customer deposits (generally 80%-85% of Indian Banks' resource base is out of Customer deposits) which are mostly repayable on demand (even Time/Fixed Deposits may be withdrawn before the date of maturity by undergoing a nominal loss of interest). Hence, a bank extending infrastructure loan always remains exposed to liquidity risk and consequent reputational risk.

In order to avert such a situation, RBI permits banks allowing infrastructure loan to have the benefit of Take-out-Finance in the following manner:

- This mechanism is to facilitate Asset-Liability maturity mismatch of financing banks for longer duration infrastructure projects of 15 years and beyond.

- After disbursing any infrastructure loan and holding the same for five years or so, a bank may face a likely situation of liquidity crunch. In that eventuality the outstanding balance may be allowed to be taken over by Infrastructural Development Finance Ltd., and/or SBI or any other financial institutions who consider such cases. However, the transferor bank must ensure that at the time of such transfer the account is held as Standard Assets in its books.
- To give effect to the aforesaid transaction necessary Stamped Agreement is to be executed by the transferor and transferee bank/institution.

INFRASTRUCTURE OPERATIONS FROM FUNDING ANGLE

Except that gestation period of an infrastructure project being fairly long there is little similarity from technical, commercial, financial and from socio-economic angle in between various infrastructure projects. Operational risks of Projects and for financing bank/institution Credit Risk elements are also not always in matching proportions.

In light of the above internationally -5- modes of infrastructure financing are prevalent:

1. Build, Operate and Transfer (BOT)
2. Build, Operate, Lease and Transfer (BOLT)
3. Build, Own, Operate and Transfer (BOOT)
4. Build, Own and Operate (BOO)
5. Build, Own, Operate and Sell (BOOS)

In India BOT (No.1) models are generally encouraged National Highway Development Programme is the largest infrastructure project in India involving an outlay of about Rs.54,000 crore. This has been undertaken on BOT Model.

BUILD, OPERATE AND TRANSFER (BOT) MODEL

BOT is a process of infrastructure development, which enables direct private sector investment in large-scale infrastructure projects especially highway, railway projects etc.

Main issues of BOT are as follows:

1. **Build:** A private company (or consortium) agrees with a government to invest in a public infrastructure project. The company then of its own initiative arranges financing for the project.

2. **Operate:** The private developer at next stage owns, maintains, and manages the project for an agreed concession period and recoups its investment through charges or toll fee etc.
3. **Transfer:** After the concessionary period the company transfers ownership and operation of the facility to the government or relevant competent authority as per the contract.

PARTIES TO BOT PROJECTS

The major parties to a BOT project are usually:

1. **Government Agency:** A government department or statutory authority is the main party. It role covers:
   - granting the sponsor the "concession", that is the right to build, own and operate the facility,
   - granting a long term lease of or sell the site to the sponsor, and
   - often acquiring most or all of the service provided by the project.
2. **Sponsor:** The sponsor is the party, usually a consortium of interested groups including a construction group, an operator, a financing institution, etc. which, in response to the invitation by the Government prepares the proposal to construct, operate, and finance, the particular project.

   The sponsor may take the form of a company, a partnership, a limited partnership, a unit trust or an unincorporated joint venture–special purpose vehicle.
3. **Construction Contractor:** The construction company may also be one of the sponsors. Its role is to take construction and completion risks, *i.e.*, the risk of completing the project on time, within budget and specifications.
4. **Operation and Maintenance Contractor:** The operator is to sign a long-term contract with the sponsor for the operation and maintenance of the project. The operator may also inject equity into the project if so necessary under any particular circumstances.
5. **Financiers:** In a large project there is likely to be a syndicate of banks financial institutions providing the debt funds to the sponsor. The same or different banks may provide a stand-by loan facility for any cost overruns not covered by the construction contract under exceptional justifiable circumstances.

SPECIAL FEATURES OF BOT MODEL

BOT Model has following major advantages:

1. The government gets the benefit of the private sector participation to mobilize finances and to use the contemporary management skills in the construction, operation and maintenance of the project.
2. The private participation also ensures speed efficiency and quality output/project by using the best available equipment and expertise.
3. The projects are mostly conducted through competitive bidding process and are thus at the lowest possible cost, without compromising any quality/standards.

BUY BACK MECHANISM

Many infrastructure projects adopt buyback mechanism as an indirect source of supply of raw materials, Machinery/equipments required for the projects. Broadly, the mechanism is as under:

- Arrangements are made that initially suppliers of raw materials, Machinery/Equipment will provide the same without receipt of cash from the infrastructure project promoters.
- However, as a consideration of supplies so made (the value of which in some projects may ever be even 30% of project cost *e.g.*, Ultra Mega Power Project) the infrastructure company allots Equity Shares to the supplier with a condition to future buyback.
- Upon implementation of the infrastructure project generating revenues the owners of the projects buyback the Equity Shares from the suppliers with a view to retain control over the enterprise.
- Presently under Indian Companies Act, restrictions have been placed on:

  (*i*) Total amount of buyback shares that can be undertaken by a company

  (*ii*) Number of shares that can be bought back in a year

  (*iii*) Borrowed funds not to be utilized for buyback.
- Deepak Parekh Committee on infrastructure has recommended relaxation of aforesaid buyback norms for infrastructure sector so as to attract private sector. Also it has recommended leveraged recapitalization for encouragement of the sector.

ESCROW ACCOUNT MECHANISM FOR INFRASTRUCTURE PROJECT

Escrow Account (legally a Trust Account) provides for a financial protective device especially in case of the infrastructure projects. The providers of service (*e.g.*, Power Generator) and buyers of the service (*e.g.*, Electricity Board) are mutually protected in their financial commitments. This mechanism is also available for other types of business transactions.

DEFINITION

There is no statutory/standardized definition of an Escrow Account. The word ESCROW implies delivery of any property/assets (money) to a Third Party (generally a Bank) who is a stranger to the transaction between two or more transacting parties. Such a third party is known as ESCROW AGENT who undertakes to deliver the property/asset to one or more of the parties eventually subject to the performance of their contractual terms.

In the Book on ESSENTIALS OF FINANCE published by THE ECONOMIST, it has been stated as under :

ESCROW Account is "A bank account kept by a third party on behalf of two others who are usually in dispute about its (*i.e.*, money deposited) rightful ownership. The disputing parties try to set out conditions under which they will agree to let the money be released. When the conditions have been met the third party releases the funds".

Examples

1. Kumar Iyer agrees to sell his land at a price of Rs.50 lac to Rahul Iyer. The vendor wants that the purchase money be deposited to a third party till all formalities for sale are completed as a protection for the buyer eventually not defaulting. For the buyer also he would not like to handover any money to seller till the transaction is completed. Hence, both Kumar Iyer and Rahul Iyer approach Good Bank Ltd., for opening of ESCROW ACCOUNT with a condition that the Bank would allow withdrawal of the amount only on receipt of confirmation from Kumar Iyer and Rahul Iyer as to the completion of Sale transaction. Thereafter Escrow Account will be closed.
2. Bharat Power Generator Co. Ltd., has agreed to supply electricity to India Electricity Board on a continuing basis provided the Board deposits at least as 5/- lac on monthly basis in an Escrow Account with Paradise Bank Ltd. The money so deposited may

be allowed to be withdrawn by Power Generator Co. (as per agreement) on confirmation from both the parties particularly about compliance of their contractual terms. Such a running Escrow Account may continue till both the parties decide to close their contract.

3. In case of international trade transaction also escrow system may arise *e.g.*, Lawson Co Ltd. (UK) agrees to supply Chemicals to Sujatha Iyer Company, India on a running basis provided the buyer first deposits the value of each shipment (say Rs.50 lac) to a Bank in India under Escrow Account. The seller sends the shipment to the buyer directly and only when the buyer confirms receipt of the shipment the bank may release the fund to the overseas seller.

FEATURES OF AN INFRASTRUCTURAL ESCROW ACCOUNT

- Escrow Account is a Trust Account with a Bank.
- The Bank will be known as Escrow Agent.
- For opening of Escrow Account the concerned parties and the Bank have to enter into a legally bounding contract known as Escrow Agreement.
- Escrow Agreement specifies role and responsibilities of the Bank and the concerned parties.
- For rendering such a special service the bank may levy service charges/fees as may be agreed under Escrow Agreement.
- Fund deposited in an Escrow Account is known as Escrow Money.
- Escrow Account mechanism is common as in case of Power, Road and telecom projects.

An Actual Case of successful Escrow

News Item at Indian Express: 30/09/2004.

Slum projects—Govt plugs loopholes

Shashank Mhasawade

MUMBAI, SEPT 30: To reign in the runaway private builders who take up housing projects under the Slum Redevelopment (SRD) scheme, the Shivshahi Punarvasan Prakalp Ltd. (SPPL), the government-owned company set up to implement the mass housing scheme, has devised a 'fool-proof' system to ensure that the State Government is not taken for a ride.

Called the Escrow Accounting Mechanism, the system will make sure projects are completed within stipulated time and the buildings meet stringent quality standards, according to senior SPPL officials.

Elaborating on the new system, a high ranking SPPL official told *The Indian Express*, "SPPL also gives loans to private developers to implement projects under the SRD scheme. The Escrow mechanism is nothing but a perfectly coordinated check and balance system involving the SPPL, the bank, the developers and the buyers of the flats. The mechanism ensures that the developer does not flee with the loan amount, leaving the project half way."

The total cost of an SRD project comprises cost of constructing transit camps, cost of rehabilitation of the slum dwellers and statutory payments by the developer to the government. Under the new mechanism, SPPL will sanction 70 per cent of this cost as a loan to the developer. Two joint accounts are then opened, in the name of SPPL and the developer's name called loan and sale account respectively.

Meanwhile, a reputed and trusted architect is appointed as its Project Management Consultant (PMC) to monitor the progress of the project. The PMC will file a mandatory report on the actual work done on the structure attaching photographs of the building from all angles and its estimated cost. This report will be in addition to the monthly project report to be submitted by the PMC.

If the PMC's cost estimate is approved, the SPPL will release only 70 per cent of the amount to the developer.

When the developer sells a flat in the free sale component in the project, the amount is deducted from the loan account to be released next time. In addition, the buyer has to draw the cheque in favour of SPPL and not in favour of the developer.

"A developer would have disappeared with the money had we not effected these controls. Unlike in other banks and government schemes, SPPL will never release the full loan amount to the developer at one go. The final payment, about 50 per cent of the cost certified by PMC, will only be released after the project is completed. Now, as he has invested his own 30 per cent amount in the first place, he will have to complete the building. The developer will have to keep the stipulated deadline or else he will not be paid," the officer said.

SPPL expects to construct about 25,000 flats under this system in the next 18 months. The company will construct 25,000 more flats on its own in the same time, the officer said.

The Escrow Accounting Mechanism is an improvised version of a real estate practice in Singapore. Instead of applying it here in toto, the SPPL officials have modified it to suit Mumbai's realestate market.

The system has already shown its results. A leading developer, who has constructed several residential complexes at Andheri, Oshiwara and

Kandivali, recently walked out of a deal with SPPL for not being able to meet the stringent provisions of the system. This, the officials claimed, has given out clear signals that developers cannot get away with cheating the government, at least not the SPPL, anymore.

❑❑❑

CHAPTER

4 Accounting Ratios in Infrastructure and the Projects*

FUNCTIONAL ROLE

A ratio conveys a quantitative inter-relationship between two attributes/ variables for eventual comparison against a benchmark for trend analysis. In business especially in infrastructure project accounting ratios facilitate meaningful and purpose-oriented decision-making from the perspective of the promoters as well as lenders and other stakeholders. Its utility is determined according to the purpose for which the ratio is computed. A commercial bank may stress more on ratios like current ratio or acid test for working capital finance, while a development financial institution may consider debt-service coverage and cash flow ratios more important. An investor for infrastructure projects may, on the other hand, consider both sets of ratios equally important.

From the angle of credit risk evaluation under infrastructure projects accounting ratios play a significant role for a lending/investing bank, since the overall computation of the credit rating of their account/exposure is aided/supported by ratio analysis also. Hence, not only is it necessary to identify relevant ratios depending on the purpose, quantum, tenure of exposure etc., but also imperative to assign weightage for the different ratios.

Internationally, there are no prescribed accounting ratios for risk evaluation applicable specially for infrastructure Units although a broad based outline may be available. In India, too, the banking regulatory authorities have left such matters to the judgement and discretion of the banks/financial institutions concerned. However, it is logical to expect a bank/financial institution to go by established financial practices in general and frame.

---

* Major portion of this Chapter is drawn from the Author's Book on Credit Risk Management.

An accounting ratio policy that is relevant to the purpose of its credit risk evaluation for infrastructure projects.

VARIOUS ACCOUNTING RATIOS AND STANDARDS FOR INFRASTRUCTURE PROCESS

For identification criteria for example, items of current assets, current liabilities, etc. – one is to be guided by Standard Accounting Practice.

1. Short-term solvency angle:

(*a*) Current ratio: $\dfrac{\text{Current assets}}{\text{Current liabilities}}$

General Minimum expected level: 2 : 1

The holding level of Current Assets and average outstanding level of accounts payable etc in infrastructure projects is very low since generally such projects are cash-driven. Hence aforesaid minimum level of 2 : 1 may be applied but in no case it should not be below 1.33 : 1.

(*b*) Acid test ratio: $\dfrac{\text{Quick assets}}{\text{Quick liabilities}}$

General Minimum expected level: 1 : 1

For infrastructure projects also above 1 : 1 ratio may be applied.

(*c*) Cash ratio: $\dfrac{\text{Cash + Bank balance + Marketable securities}}{\text{Current liabilities}}$

General Minimum expected level: 0.5 : 1

For infrastructure sectors etc. the minimum level may be generally to atleast 0.6 : 1

2. Long-term solvency angle:

Debt Equity Ratio: $\dfrac{\text{Total external liabilities}}{\text{Equity (owned funds)}}$

General Maximum allowable level: 2 : 1

While it is often observed that in infrastructure projects overall Debt Equity ratio is 60 : 40, Power Projects have higher at 68 : 32. Lowest is generally in telecom sector at 50 : 50.

General Minimum expected level: 1.50 : 1

Infrastructure Projects should also in general confirm to above minimum level.

3. Profitability angle:

(*a*) Operating profit ratio:

$$\frac{\text{Profit before deduction of depreciation, tax and finance charges}}{\text{Sales/income}}$$

The expected level will depend upon the nature of the industry/business, operational area, size of the unit, the duration of the business being carried on, trend analysis and other relevant factors. However, a good unit is likely to show at least a margin of 25–30%.

(*b*) return on capital employed (ROCE) ratio:

$$\frac{\text{Operating profit}}{\text{Owned funds + Long-term loan funds}}$$

The expected level will be based on factors as stated in 3(*a*) above. However, ordinarily it is likely to be at least 15–20%.

(*c*) Interest coverage ratio: $\frac{\text{Operating profit}}{\text{Interest liability}}$

Subject to factors as stated in 3(*a*) above.

(*d*) Profit-asset ratio: $\frac{\text{Operating profit}}{\text{Total tangible assets}}$

The minimum expected level will depend upon factors as stated in 3(*a*) above.

(*e*) Indirect overhead ratio:

$$\frac{\text{Finance charges + Depreciation (on fixed assets for administrative/office purposes) + Selling and administrative cost}}{\text{Sales/income}}$$

The maximum allowable level is to be decided on a case-by-case basis based on 3(*a*) above. However, it may be 10–15%.

4. From the asset movement angle:

(*a*) $\frac{\text{Inventory holding} \times \text{300 days**}}{\text{Sales/Income}}$

(*b*) $\frac{\text{Trade debtors} \times \text{300 days** (preferably average outstanding in a year)}}{\text{Sales/Income}}$

5. Trade credit payment angle:

$$\frac{\text{Trade creditors} \times 300 \text{ days}^{**} \text{ (preferably average outstanding in a year)}}{\text{Credit purchase of current assets (preferably) average level in a year}}$$

** Computation based on 300 days in a year is advisable in the Indian context keeping in view the usual 52 weekly offs, national holidays, etc.

The expected level varies from case to case as stated in 3(*a*) above. However, generally, the maximum level in terms of days may be between 90 and 120.

6. From the 'stress' angle: (The Basel Committee on Risk Management states: "Stress testing has been adopted as a generic term describing various techniques used by banks to gauge their potential vulnerability to exceptional, but plausible, events.")

$$\frac{\text{Stress tested cash flow}}{\text{Debt payments + Preference dividend + Interest}}$$

For this purpose, cash flow would include only operating cash flow (ignoring investing cash flow and financing cash flow). As a point of the stress testing scale, a reduction of a certain percentage in income/sales with a simultaneous increase in expense (for example, direct costs, etc) may result in charge (reduction) in cash flow. There is no minimum or maximum. The stress percentage depends on the industry, and in case of infrastructure projects whether the one is physical infrastructure or social infrastructure operating environment, and also the overall business environment at the time of analysis.

OFF-BEAT ACCOUNTING RATIOS (ESPECIALLY APPLICABLE FOR MNCs INVOLVED IN R&D INTENSIVE PROJECTS)

- Of late business expansion of Corporates across national boundaries take place frequently. Large number of MNCs (Multi National Corporations) Operate in India as their base office with wings spread over a number of countries. In consequence, conventional accounting ratios need to be supplemented by various other ratios for the purpose of a more meaningful analysis of financial position of such MNC.
- Some off-beat accounting ratios (as under) applicable for analysis of annual financial statements of MNCs especially those involved in R&D intensive goods have come into being.

1. ROY Ratio (Ratio of Royalty Payment to Net Sales Turnover):

$$\text{ROY} = \frac{\text{Annual Royalty Payment}}{\text{Net Sales}}$$

2. LP Ratio (Lump Payment for import of technology to Net-Sales):

$$= \frac{\text{LP}}{\text{Net Sales}}$$

3. MK Ratio (Import of capital goods to Net Sales):

$$\text{MK} = \frac{\text{Annual of Import of Capital Goods (by the Co)}}{\text{Net-sales}}$$

4. M RAW Ratio (Import of Raw Materials and Stores to Net Sales):

$$\text{M RAW} = \frac{\text{Annual Cost of Raw-materials and Stores}}{\text{Net Sales}}$$

5. AGE Ratio (The age of MNC measured by total amount of Depreciation reserve to Gross Fixed Assets):

$$= \frac{\text{Total Depreciation Reserves}}{\text{Gross Fixed Assets}}$$

NOTES

(*a*) No standard ratio of the above five has so far been arrived at and used.

(*b*) Owing to a number of variables in operations the aforesaid off-beat ratio may vary from one MNC to another MNC. Hence, the analyst should take a total view of financial data of the MNC and arrive at the conclusion. However, year-to-year favourable/unfavourable variations in movements are to be captured in MNC's overall accounting ratio framework and then draw conclusion on the well-being or otherwise of MNC.

The lending bankers/financial institutions are yet to implement such off-beat ratios in their credit appraisal process in all cases.

The above cluster is only indicative of the ratios which may be applied for infrastructure sectors that a commercial bank/financial institution may find useful from the credit risk evaluation angle. There may be other important ratios as well, such as:

- Cash flow interest coverage
- Capital gearing ratio
- Proprietory ratio

Here's some wise advice from Rally & Brown: "You can envision a large number of potential financial ratio through which to examine almost every possible relationship. The trick is not to come up with more ratios but to attempt to limit the number of ratios so that you can examine them in a meaningful way." (Investment Analysis and Portfolio Management, 6th Edition, page 429).

Accounting ratios are usually computed on the year-end position of assets, liabilities, profit/loss account components (over a position of generally 12 months) as reflected in the actual financial statements and/or projected data/information. This is based on a 'going concern' approach. However, one limitation here is that the 'static' view of assets and liabilities at the end of the year may not reflect the true and correct position. The alternative is to collect the figures from the party concerned, say, on a monthly basis (or as frequently as may be possible) and average the same on a 12-month basis. This may then, for credit risk evaluation purposes, be a more effective and dynamic too. Irrespective of whether a bank/financial institution follows the year-end or average method of computation, the implications from the credit risk evaluation angle will depend upon:

- Adopting an appropriate credit rating system with generally a large number of grades, where one of the inputs would be accounting ratios.
- The bank/financial institution will have to decide as a matter of corporate finance policy the nature of the accounting ratios to be used for credit risk evaluation (for example, there may be a different focus in assessing working capital for loans for fixed assets or for non-funded facilities/investment in securities, etc.). For infrastructure sector Term Loan and Non-funded facilities are predominant issues.
- Specific weights have to be allocated for accounting ratios (from the credit rating angle). Say, 20 out of a total of 100 points for the entire credit rating structure.
- The benchmarking for each ratio should be consistent with the bank's/financial institution's corporate finance policy.
- The maximum weightage for each component of the ratio should be fixed–say, 4 out of 20 points (20 being the total for all accounting ratios put together).
- Ratios conforming to the benchmark should be awarded the highest points. Those below the benchmark should be ranked with varying points, down to even zero.
- Total marks awarded for all adopted ratios should then be carried forwarded to the overall credit rating structure so as to arrive at final grade for each account/exposure.

INSURANCE ELEMENT IN ACCOUNTING RATIO

Although a powerful tool in credit risk evaluation, ratio analysis is not, however, the only criterion. There are a number of other parameters on which credit risk is analysed, like asset cover (credit mitigants as per Basel terminology), management quality of the borrowing party, macro-economic indicators that have an impact on the exposure, etc. and for infrastructure projects special focus on 'welfare' aspect. Ratio analysis is not an insurance against credit risk because of the following:

- Each ratio is indicative of a certain aspect of the organisation. For example, current ratio is with respect to current assets and current liabilities only. It's not possible to look at the total picture from this.
- A favourable ratio may indicate poor performance on another dimension. For example a current ratio of over 2 : 1 (say 3 : 1) may show the management's inefficiency in holding current assets idle, with the accompanying carrying costs.
- Ratio analysis is an overwhelming reflection of past position. The same position may or may not hold in the future which is fraught with uncertainty especially in infrastructure projects.
- The computation of the ratio depends on the analyst's views, approach, perception and objectivity, particularly while identifying the components of a ratio. For example, while identifying current assets, some analysts may not consider certain assets as being 'current' (like inventory lying in stock beyond a particular period) or treat some liabilities as being 'current', although they may be classified as a term liability (like sundry unsecured loans without any specific repayment schedule).
- As far as ratio test is concerned, an analogy may be drawn with medical pathology. The blood report of an individual may show an ideal level of Haemoglobin on the date of the test, which may drastically change soon after some adverse physiological developments. In the same way, ratio analysis may not provide any guarantee about the quality of credit assets on a continuous basis.

Keeping all these limitations in mind, it may be said that credit risk protection can come from a combination factors, and not from an isolated (ratio) one. Nevertheless, accounting ratios still play a dominant role in credit risk evaluation.

❑❑❑

CHAPTER

5 Credit Rating for Infrastructure Projects*

Credit Rating implies an assessment/evaluation of a particular credit proposition – funded as well as non-funded on the basis of credit parameters such as performance analysis, management quality and market scenario, etc. with scores under each parameter. The aggregate score in an account as against overall score reflects the strength/ weakness of the respective account.

BASEL COMMITTEE of Bank for International Settlements (Central Bank of Central Banks of countries) has **defined** Credit Rating as under:

> "....a summary indicator of the risk inherent in an individual credit and embodies an assessment of the risk of loss due to the default of counter party on consideration of relevant quantitative and qualitative information."

UTILITY OF CREDIT RATING FOR INFRASTRUCTURE PROJECTS

Credit Rating is an important tool for assessment of any credit account as well as for undertaking post-disbursement monitoring and follow up. In this respect, Basel Committee considers that as Credit Rating facilitates monitoring of credit risk, the system to be in place in each Bank should be integrated into an institution's overall analysis of credit risk and capital adequacy. The system should be strong enough to support the identification and measurement of risk from credit exposures in light of the fact that exposures in Infrastructure process are huge and are on fairly of long duration.

---

* Some portion of the Chapter has been drawn from the Author's existing publications.

In this context the utility of Credit Rating may be viewed from the following aspects for an infrastructure project:

- Evaluation of the borrower in totality.
- Transaction level analysis, credit pricing and tenure.
    1. Activity-wise/sector-wise portfolio study keeping in view macro level position.
    2. Fixation of outer limit of taking up/maintaining an exposure arising out of risk rating-scope for take-out after initial booking period of 3-5 years.
    3. Monitoring of existing exposures and to decide safety strategies in appropriate cases.
    4. Allocation of risk capital (economic capital) in cases of poor-graded accounts.
    5. Avoidance of over concentration of exposure in specific risk grades.

In short, such a Credit Rating mechanism enables :

(*i*) Bifurcation of accounts into graded risk attributes.

(*ii*) Pricing of credit based on risk grade.

(*iii*) Focusing higher order attention for monitoring poorly graded accounts.

USUAL METHOD OF CREDIT RATING

Michel Cronhy *et al* considers that an appropriate method of Credit Rating must satisfy following aspects:

1. It must generate accurate information base.
2. It must facilitate consistent evaluation.
3. It must provide flexibility to allow professional judgement to significantly influence a rating.

The following Two Methods are prescribed in Credit Rating system depending upon the suitability of one method in a particular case:

1. **Through the Cycle Mehtod:** Under this method, the financial position of the borrower and/or position of exposure is assessed, assuming "worst point in business cycle". Element of subjectivity of the evaluator may influence in grading an account.
2. **Point-in-Time Method:** A rating system based on "Current Condition" of the borrower/exposure is done under Point-in-Time method. For assessing such current condition, financial statements, current market position or trade/business, overall management expertise are all taken into account for rating under this method.

In respect of infrastructure projects Point-in-Time Method should be adopted in view of the following reasons:

- It is simple in adoption while it has all the safeguards in-built.
- It can be applied consistently and objectively to generate a fair estimate of risk grade of an account.
- It has the flexibility of periodical review depending upon the eventual outcome of grade accounts.

USUAL PARAMETERS FOR CREDIT RATING

It is very important to select appropriate parameters, if a Credit Rating system has to be effective, since the scores under each parameter when aggregated will reflect grading of an account. The set of parameters to be taken may be broadly divided into:

- Quantitative Parameters
- Qualitative Parameters

Qualitative Parameters are:

(*i*) How the unit is conforming to any regulatory norm, *e.g.*, negative grants/Revenue Sharing.

(*ii*) Experience of the Top Management of the unit in various activities of the business.

(*iii*) Initiative of Top Management in staying ahead of competitors.

(*iv*) Honouring financial commitments.

(*v*) End-use of borrowed funds.

(*vi*) Firm's ability to cope up with major technological, regulatory and legal changes, if any.

On the other hand, **Quantitative Parameters** are with regard to actual/projected business performance of the borrower as under :

- Growth in Gross income year-on-year.
- Growth in Operating Profit, Net Profit year-on-year.
- Return on Capital employed.
- Debt-Equity Ratio.
- Debt Service Coverage Ratio.
- Current Ratio.
- Speed of debt collection/revenue collection.
- Level of contingent liabilities.
- Security offered/available.

In short, Business Performance, Financial Performance, Conduct of Account and Security aspects are considered major aspects.

In practice, each Bank, depending upon its Corporate Policy decides the nature of parameters and weightage for each parameter with the ultimate objective, however, to use the Credit Rating tool as the facilitator for risk grading of each account. For infrastructure projects the following model of parameters may be adopted by a bank/financial institutions.

SPECIMEN FORMAT

There is no standardized format of Credit Rating. Each Bank devises its Bank-specific format for its borrowers. The following format and methodology may be appropriate:

S.No.	Parameter			
	SECTION A: MARKS RANGE FOR BUSINESS POTENTIALS			
1.	Market Potential – Demand/Supply position for the product/service	Favourable (4)	Neutral (2)	Unfavourable (0)
2.	Diversification of products service among different consumer/area	Favourable (4)	Neutral (2)	Unfavourable (0)
3.	Cyclicality/Seasonality of the product service dealt	Low (4)	Moderate (2)	High (0)
4.	Chances of Obsolescence of business activity/services	Low (4)	Moderate (2)	High (0)
5.	Competition in the line of business activity	Favourable (4)	Neutral (2)	Unfavourable (0)
6.	Location of the Unit/Establishment from Commercial/Servicing angle	Favourable (4)	Neutral (2)	Unfavourable (0)
7.	Experience of the promoters in the same line of activity.	More than 3 year (4)	One year to 3 years (2)	Less than 1 year (0)

Max. Marks		Marks Obtained		
	SECTION–B: MARKS RANGE FOR FINANCIAL PERFORMANCE**			
1.	Achievement of projected turnover/ Gross Income	Achieved (4)	Upto 75% less than 100% (2)	Below 75% (0)
2.	Achievement of projected net profit before tax	Achieved (4)	Upto 75% Less than 100% (2)	Below 75% (0)

3.	Growth in Gross over the previous year	Above 10% positive growth (4)	0 to 10% positive growth (2)	No growth/ Negative growth (0)
4.	Increase in Net profit before tax over previous year	Above 10% increase (4)	0 to 10% increase (2)	No increase (0)
5.	Current Ratio	1.33 & above (4)	Below 1.33 to 1.17 (2)	Below 1.17 (0)
6.	Total outside Liability/Eqity	Below 2 (4)	2 to 3 (2)	Over 3 (0)

** For new Unti-2-marks may be awarded.

Max. Score			Score Obtained	
SECTION–C: CONDUCT OF ACCOUNT (EXISTING PROJECTS)**				
1.	Honouring commitment to Bank for payment of interest, instalments etc.	Timely within 7 days (4)	Delayed but within 1 month (2)	Delayed beyond one month (0)
2.	Irregularities in the conduct of	No return during (4)	Not more than-2-returns (2)	More than-2-returns (0)
3.	Excess Drawings (excluding due to interest application – (During last -6- months)	No excess drawing (4)	Not more than-2-excess drawing (2)	More than-2-excess drawing (0)
4.	Non-retirement of bills under L/C (During last one year)	Timely within 10 days (4)	Delayed but within 1 month (2)	Delayed beyond 1 month (0)
5.	Invocation of Guarantee (During last one year)	No Invocation (4)	—	Invocation (0)
6.	Routing of sales through us	Above 75% (4)	50% to 75% (2)	(0)
7.	Compliance of Terms and conditions	Fully complied (4)	—	Partial compliance/ Non-compliance (0)

** For new Unit -2- marks may be awarded.

	Max. Score		Score Obtained	
SECTION–C: CONDUCT OF ACCOUNT (EXISTING PROJECTS)**				
8.	Submission of Control Statements – as per terms of sanction	Timely (4)	Delayed but within 15 days (2)	Submitted beyond 15 days (0)
9.	Submission of financial statements as per terms of sanction	Submitted one month before due date of review (4)	Submitted before due date of review (2)	Submitted after due date of review (0)
10.	Relationship with us	Over 3 years (4)	One year to 3 years (2)	Less than 1 year (0)

	Max. Score		Marks Obtained	
SECTION–D: SECURITY				
1.	Marketability of primary security	Good (2)	Average Poor (1)	Very Low/ (0)
2.	Durability of primary security	Good (2)	Average (1)	Very Low/ Poor (0)
3.	Price stability of primary security	Good (2)	Average (1)	Very Low/ Poor (0)
4.	Type of collateral security	Property/ Paper security (2)	Machinery and other fixed assets (1)	Current Assets/No collateral (0)
5.	Coverage of collateral security	100% and above (4)	Below 100% but upto 50 (2)	Below 50% (0)
6.	Marketability of collateral security	Good (2)	Average (1)	Very Low/ Poor (0)
7.	Price stability of collateral security	Good (2)	Average (1)	Very Low/ Poor (0)

** For new Unit -2- marks may be awarded

	Max. Score		Marks Obtained	
SECTION–D: SECURITY				
8.	Convenience of Ascertainment of tile	High (2)	Moderate (1)	Low (0)
9.	Convenience of transferability of title (sale)	High (2)	Moderate (1)	Low (0)
10.	Ownership of Collateral Security	Borrower's name (4)	Jointly with Borrower's name (4)	Third party's name (0)

Sec.	Definition of Section	Max. Score	Score obtained
A	Business Potential		
B	Financial Performance		
C	Conduct of Account		
D	Security		

Credit Rating Grades

Grade No.	Nature of Grade	Score relating to Grade%**	Definition of the Grade
1.	AAA	85–100%	Highest Safety
2.	AA	80–84%	Very High Safety
3.	AA –	75–79%	High Safety
4.	A +	70–74%	Adequate Safety
5.	A –	65–69%	Moderate Safety
6.	BBB	60–64%	Marginal Safety
7.	BB +	50–59%	Low Safety or Risk Prone
8.	BB –	40–49%	Substandard or High Probability of default
9.	BB	30–39%	Doubtful or very high probability of default
10.	B	0–29%	Loss or highest probability of default

** For new Unit 5% - 10% discount factor may be provided for grading purpose.

STEPS CREDIT RATING FOR INFRASTRUCTURE PROJECTS TO BE UNDERTAKEN

Step 1: To decide various Risk Grades.

As per RBI guidelines a Credit Rating System should be broadly as under:

- Rating Scale may consist of 9 levels.
- Of the above, first 5 levels may represent acceptable credit risk and the remaining 4 levels as unacceptable credit risk.
- Rating Scales may be in number, *e.g.*, 1, 2, etc. or alphabet AAA, AA, etc. Basel Accord-II has, however, indicated rating scales in alphabets as under:
  - (*i*) AAA
  - (*ii*) AA
  - (*iii*) AA–
  - (*iv*) A+
  - (*v*) A
  - (*vi*) A–
  - (*vii*) BBB+
  - (*viii*) BBB
  - (*ix*) BB
  - (*x*) BB–
  - (*xi*) Below BB (Say B)
  - (*xii*) Unrated

Step 2: To devise parameters and score for each parameter.

Step 3: To devise score for each Grade.

Step 4: To decide about periodicity of Credit Rating of each account. It may be annual/half-yearly/quarterly.

IS THERE ANY NEED FOR UNDERTAKING CREDIT RATING SINCE ALL INFRASTRUCTURE PROJECT FUNDINGS ARE BACKED BY EXTENSIVE VIABILITY STUDIES?

The dimensions of viability study reports and Credit Rating exercises may contain some common elements like business potential, financial and other allied issues. But credit rating is still to be treated as a distinct utility tool in view mainly of the following reasons:

- Evaluation of overall Credit risk is aimed at while assessing specific risk elements having regard to international principles of risk management (BASEL II).
- Credit Rating facilitates decision making process of the lending or not – if yes, to what extent and with what risk mitigation avenues.
- Credit rating views strength and weakness of the borrower/project parameter-wise without unduly focusing on overall aspects of the borrower/project.
- Credit rating enables Commercial Pricing of Credit – highly rated credit proportion may command lowest pricing as against others.
- Credit Rating is not an one-time exercise (like viability studies) and is an ongoing periodical process depending upon the nature of project, amount of exposure etc.

Thus, there is no substitute for credit rating in any lending process for infrastructure project.

❑❑❑

CHAPTER

6 Techniques of Infrastructure Lending

As per regulatory prescription any credit facility whether funded (*e.g.*, Loan/Overdraft etc.) or non-funded (*e.g.*, Letter of Credit/Guarantee etc.) extended to any party engaged in developing or operating and maintaining or a combination of all the aforesaid is eligible to be classified as infrastructure leading. The national priority/focus and concessions in finance cost and/ or tax concessions would, in the process, apply to such sectoral exposures.

It may, however, be stressed here that even though infrastructure sector deserves all the thrust and attention in the national interest, there cannot be any let-up in matters of applying the cardinal principles of Lending appraisal and post disbursement monitoring and follow-up. Infrastructure projects being capital intensive and of long gestation nature with possibilities of time and cost over runs, obviously, higher intensity risk implications arise in funding infrastructure projects. Hence, banks/financial institutions should take all protective measures by way of 'Caution' but must always have 'open mind' because of social value of such projects.

BASIC GUIDE POSTS

Lending techniques for infrastructural projects have to be broad-based and well focused in view mainly of the following factors:

- Quantum of finance usually required is very large – in crores generally.
- Repayment period is usually very long – generally 15 years + with long moratorium of 3 years + in many cases.
- Revenue generations and achievement of surplus is dependent upon a variety of socio-politico factors especially in case of relatively huge utilities such as domestic power usage, telecom, Highway etc.
- Tangible securities for the exposure are of large book value Capital assets but not always possible for smooth disposal in the event of necessities for recovery of defaulted amount of loan/advance if any without undergoing ‘Critical Fire-sale’, *i.e.*, absolutely at a large quantum of loss should at all any buyer be available.

- While pricing of services such as power tariff, toll charge etc. may be subject to regulatory control (because of socio-economic implications), overheads such as maintenance charges, and other business overheads may often surprisingly go up, creating a major mismatch between original planned net cash-flows and actuals from time to time. This may affect servicing of financial commitments.

In view of all the above a full scale Due Diligence study is required to be undertaken while processing a proposal for infrastructure lending with attention to the following Guideposts:

1. Promoter/Management Perspective
2. Technical Perspective
3. Commercial Perspective
4. Financial Perspective
5. Socio-economic Impact Perspective

1. Promoter/Management Perspective

(*A*) Complete track record of the Promoters/Organisations and their past dealings and account relationships with banks/financial institutions, if any should be thoroughly ascertained. The promoters may be of first generation entrepreneurs or already recognised/ reputed persons in the market/society.

In the context of background study following aspects should be kept in view:

- Family background, academic/professional qualifications, age.
- Details of sources of income.
- Copies of Income Tax Reforms/Certificates wherever applicable.
- Copies of Wealth Tax Returns for last 3 years if applicable.
- Names/addresses of banks where personal/family accounts of promoters are maintained.

(*B*) As regards the borrowing organisation following aspects are to be ascertained:

- If the organisation is a Corporate Unit, Memorandum and Articles of Association should be examined to ensure that proposed infrastructures activity is within the objects clause of the Memorandum.
- Amount of Authorised Capital/Paid up Capital.
- Borrowing power and provision of offering the securities of the company as cover to banks/financial institutions.
- Full details of Board of Directors in case of Limited Companies and Board of Management in case of others.

- Whether there is any clause in borrower's charters/other documents for appointment of institutional Nominee.
- Extent of Promoters' financial contribution and representation on the board, sharing of responsibilities.
- Procedure if any for divestment of their interest if warranted.
- Corporate strategic plan of the borrower for next 3-5 years.
- Particulars of other Projects promoted/implemented if any.
- Present status of Infrastructure project under implementation.
- Details of Group Companies if any, overall view of their operations and financial commitments.

(*C*) Details of Top Management and other responsibilities.

- Name, Qualification and Experience of Chief Executive Officer/ Chief Operating Officer and Chief Financial Officer and pay details as applicable.

2. Technical Perspective: Following aspects need special attention:

- In case the project involves installation of Power Station, School/ College, Hospital etc., distance from nearest railway station, port and airport.
- Adequacy of staff housing facilities in case of construction new roads, power projects etc.
- Particulars of land and how suitable for the project keeping in view of special characteristics of project.
- Tentative amount of land development costs.
- Whether soil/water test reports confirm suitability of project especially in case of drinking water projects.
- Whether technology proposed to be used in the project is proven one.
- Performance data of other projects based on same technology.
- Possibility of risk of obsolescence of technology in near future.
- Track record of licensor of technology.
- Right of sub-licensor to transfer technology/basic engineering.
- Likely amount of annual license fee, royalty, exclusivity of licence.
- Flow chart and description of project implementation/continuation-nature of contract: engineering, procurement and construction/turnkey etc.
- Whether competitive bids where mandatory were invited.
- Experience of Contractor/Consultant in similar infrastructure projects.

- Gist of major terms of agreement with the contractor especially in respect of premature cancellation.
- Whether performance guarantee from a scheduled bank for timely completion of assigned project work with laid down norms, quality etc. will be available.
- List of machinery, equipments, other capital assets with copies of proforma invoices.
- To what extent plant capacity (mainly applicable for power projects) is comparable from international plant size angle.
- Strength and experience of internal project monitoring them constituted/ to be constituted.
- Role and responsibilities of Consultants, Contractor and Project team.
- Availability of imported spare parts (if necessary) and other items that may be necessary on an ongoing basis for the project.
- Risk involved in sustained supply of spare parts/other items of daily necessity for the project.
- Staff Competence (-managerial, supervisory-flow level staff) with likely amount of monthly wage costs.
- Ready availability of key personnel in case of any contingency.
- Status of other projects, if any, already undertaken.
- Project period covering erection, installation and commissioning.

3. Commercial Perspective: In any project venture Commercial aspects center round potential market demand for the product/services proposed to be the output of the project and possible future scenario in the supply-demand framework. Infrastructure projects being utility items/services for mass welfare are to be treated generally as commercially viable projects with state incentives where applicable (low power tariff for poor people, free medicine/hospital services, free schooling etc.). However, this should not be construed to suggest that infrastructure projects should always be a burden of state exchequer. Where possible such projects must be on self supporting basis with differential service/price mechanism as may be appropriate on case to case basis.

4. Financial Perspective: Cost of Project, Means of Finance and profitability estimate are the pre-dominant issues in the analysis of Financial-viability as explained below:

(*A*) Cost of land should be as per actual price evidenced by Conveyance Deed/Agreement with the vendors which, of course, should be matching the prevalent market rates.

- There may be cases of cost implications towards resettlement of displaced inhabitants (especially in case of road, airport construction) which should also be taken into accounts.
- In light of specific infrastructure project situations having bearing of uneven meteorological conditions, additional cost factor should be built in the project estimates.
- Cost of Plant of Machinery, equipments should be strictly as per proforma invoices. International bidding procedure is generally the guiding base for cost estimate for fixed assets in case of infrastructure projects.
- Cost estimate for erection and commissioning, taxes, insurance, freight together with provision for foundation, installation, piping, insulation charges must be reasonable having regard to similar projects.
- Provision of inflation impact of 15%–20% of Cost of Machinery, equipments etc. should be built in the project cost.
- Justification of technical know-how fees, if any should be studied. If there is any provision for visit of any technician, cost thereof should also be incorporated in the project.
- Cost for miscellaneous items of fixed assets, *e.g.*, furniture, office equipments, computer systems, vehicles etc. should also be provided.
- Preliminary and Pre-operative expenses, legal expenses, Project Report fees etc. should also be provided for in this project.
- Margin Money (generally 25% if working capital requirements) requirement is an item of cost of project. While in case of infrastructure projects, requirement of working capital finance is limited, appropriate Margin Money provision should be in-built in the project.

(*B*) Proposed financing Window of the project should be examined in light of following issues:

- Paid up share capital (owned fund).
- There should be an appropriate combination of share capital and debt finance (an infrastructure project without any provision for debt fund hardly seen). While a larger proportion by share capital is welcome, from tax angle implications of debt fund should be examined case by case so as to ensure higher shareholder value (usually share capital and debt component is in the ratio of 30 : 70).

- Unsecured loan from promoters/group if any, should normally be interest-free and subordinated to any loan from bank/financial institution. In case for any justifiable reason interest is to be paid for such loans it must be ensured that rate of interest is lower than that of institutional loans.
- When the project provides for recourse to Term Loan from different lenders (in case of infrastructure projects generally on Consortium/Syndication basis), it must be ensured that necessary tie-up amongst is made in process.
- Where Government subsidy/grants are expected but only at the stage of commencement of operations etc., the project must provide for interim source of finance adjustable on receipt of subsidy/grant.
- Examination of Profitability estimates is also a key area in the matter of financial perspective. Projected Profit/Loss Accounts, Balance Sheet, Cash Flow statements etc. need a thorough study keeping in view the following main issues:
  (*i*) Unit sale price of Product/Services.
  (*ii*) Sensitivity analysis with reasonable provision of adding up estimated cost say by 10% or reducing estimated revenue say by 10% or so and thereafter to reassess viability of the project.
- Internal Rate of Return (IRR) is to be worked out based on discounted cash inflows generally spread over 15 years for Infrastructure projects. Analysis should be made for both pre-tax and post-tax IRR.

5. Socio-Economic Impact Perspective: While aforesaid four perspectives (Promoter/Management, Technological, Commercial, Financial) are intended to evaluate in the ultimate analysis for the benefit of the owners/shareholders, any infrastructure needs also to keep vigilant eye on the benefit to the society at large. In this context following analysis is quite relevant for infrastructure projects:

- Economic Rate of Return (ERR) provides the rate of discount which equates the real economic project cost to its real economic benefits. Both projects costs (based international/'shadow' prices) and project benefits should be on the basis of international price-level.
- Domestic Resource Cost (DRC) and Effective Rate of Protection (ERP):

DRC is to judge in light of Indian rupee *vis-à-vis* US Dollar for the investment in the project. ERP, on the other hand, shows the extent of protection allowed/likely to be allowed to a project and to what extent the project is competitive under a set of prices (costs).

CRITERIA FOR FINANCING: RBI DIRECTIVE

RBI has advised Banks/Financial Institutions that they may finance infrastructure projects under Public Sector/Private Sector undertakings. This should be in conformity with normal lending standards and, in particular, following aspects must be complied with:

(*i*) Project must be technically feasible; financially viable and bankable.

(*ii*) Amount of Loan/Advances should be with single borrower exposure ceiling of 15% + 5%, *i.e.*, total 20% bank's capital fund and in case of Group exposure: 40% + 10%, *i.e.*, total.

(*iii*) Comprehensive risk analysis and sensitivity analysis and entire project appraisal must be undertaken by the competent officials in the Financing Bank/Financial Institutions.

(*iv*) While extending term Loan and/or investment in Bonds etc. to projects undertaken by Public Sector Units including Public Sector Special Purpose Vehicles (SPVs) incorporated under Indian Companies Act, it must be ensured that the Loan "should not be in lieu of or to substitute budgetary resources envisaged in the project. However, where no such budgetary provision exists in the project outlay, term loan may be made available.

(*v*) The lending Bank/Financial Institution must ensure by appropriate Due Diligence study that revenues from the project would be in a position to meet debt servicing obligations (periodic repayment of loan/repayment of Bond amount) without relying on any budgetary support. Funding is to be only for specific monitorable projects.

(*vi*) Financing Private Sector SPVs for financially viable infrastructure project is also permissible but care must be taken to "that the bankruptcy or financial difficulties of the parent/sponsor should not affect the financial health of SPV" .

APPRAISAL STANDARDS: RBI DIRECTIVE

Appraisal of a lending proposition implies a thorough examination of the quality of the application in the context of basic guide posts explained earlier – insofar as all-time safety of funds of – lenders is concerned coupled with for obvious reasons a fair return in the form of Interest/Fees etc.

The foremost objective of the appraisal process is to ensure that project estimates in terms of sales/main income and post tax profit (after providing for all financial and business overheads) would be sufficient with a reasonable margin of safety.

In case of Infrastructural lending for new projects, in particular, the analysis has to be in light of projected data/information possibility of inter-firm comparison is very rare. Thus, it all depends on the skill and competence of the appraiser/team as to how an appraised project would deliver at the backdrop of estimates made.

Since infrastructure lending proposals are of very high value running into crores, it is generally advisable to finance such projects jointly by a multiple of leaders under Consortium/Syndication arrangement. This would, besiding spreading the contours of inherent financial risks, provide for joint expertise and wisdom both at the pre-sanction stage and during post-disbursement stage and ultimate repayment of the Loan/advance.

RBI directive in the matter of appraisal of infrastructural lending proposal is as under:

"(*i*) In respect of financing of infrastructure projects under taken by Government owned entities, Banks/Financial Institutions should undertake due diligence on the viability of the projects. Banks should ensure that the individual components of financing and returns on the project are well defined and assessed Government guarantees may not be taken as a substitute for satisfactory credit appraisal and such appraisal requirements should not be diluted on the basis of any reported arrangement with the Reserve Bank of India or any bank for regular standing instructions/ periodic payment instructions for servicing loans/bonds.

(*ii*) Infrastructure projects are often financed through Special Purpose Vehicles. Financing of these projects would, therefore call for special appraisal skills on the part of lending agencies. Identification of various project risks, evaluation of risk mitigation through appraisal of project contracts and evaluation of creditworthiness of the contracting entities and their abilities to fulfill contractual obligations will be an integral part of the appraisal exercise. In this connection, Banks/FIs may consider constituting appropriate screening committees/special cells for appraisal of credit proposals and monitoring progress/performance of the projects. Often, the size of the funding requirement would necessitate joint financing Banks/FIs or financing by more than one bank under consortium or syndication arrangements. In such cases, participating Banks/

FIs may, for the purpose of their own assessment, refer to the appraisal report prepared by the lead Bank/FI or have the project appraised jointly."

VIABILITY STUDIES BY APPROVED CONSULTANTS

The feasibility of project estimates on which a lending decision is based is of utmost importance both for the lenders and the borrowers. Keeping in view the fact that infrastructural projects are voluminous in terms of size, monetary involvement, gestation period and various operational risk issues, it is always desirable that the would be borrower arrange an exhaustive Project Report from approved Consultants. Usually Banks/ Financial Institutions maintain a list of such approved Consultants. The job of the Consultant interalia involves:

- Study of entire technical, commercial, including Projected Balance Sheet (*i.e.*, Project/Loss Account) and Fund Flow analysis; Managerial and Socio-economic aspects.
- Draw conclusions on each of the above aspects.
- Suggest remedial measures if any of the estimate at any point of time turns out to be unfavourable.

In actual practice the promoters of their own engage project consultants for Viability Report and approach Banks/Financial Institutions for financial assistance if Viability Report is satisfactory. In case such a consultant is not on the approved list of the bank/financial institution, such a viability report need not be acted upon for the purpose of the credit proposal. However, it must be clearly mentioned to the promoters that even a satisfactory report from their approved Consultant does not confer any right of financial assistance from the concerned bank/financial institution even in cases where a bank/financial institutions refers any such case to their consultants at the request and cost of the would-be borrower.

Upon receipt of any viability report from approved Consultant the job of the bank/financial institution involves:

- Objective in-house review of the project estimated by their Competent officials.
- In case their observations do not match with those of the consultant a reference is to be made to the would-be borrower for clarification. If satisfactory reply is received, further processing may be taken up.
- Arising out of any such internal studies by the bank/financial institutions, it may often be necessary to suggest piecemeal implementation of the project and thereby to spread over the funding provided such piecemeal implementation is found workable.

- Bank/Financial institutions must always treat a viability report as only a rough guide but not a safety valve under any circumstances.

MODALITY OF COMPUTATION OF NEED-BASED FINANCIAL ACCOMMODATION

1. **For Loan/Deferred Payment Guarantee for Fixed Assets:** The Project Viability Report (for new unit) will show the details of fixed assets required with tentative values. For existing units, going in for expansion, it is also to be ensured that a Viability Report is available showing similar information.

Where, however, for any justifiable reason say for financing a small value equipment etc. Project Viability Report has not been obtained, the applicant will have to explain to the satisfaction of bank/financial institutions the basis of computing the requirement of fixed assets and how viability is ensured especially in the context of servicing the financial commitment for acquiring the asset.

When the Bank is satisfied with the need and all aspects of viability of the Project with special emphasis on repayment capacity as may be assessed through Fund Flow/Other Financial statement the next stages would be as under:

- Normally, borrowers are expected to put in at least 25% of their funds towards acquisition of fixed assets as margin money. Hence, Bank is only expected to finance balance 75%, *e.g.*, if cost of assets to be acquired is Rs.10 crore, loan from Bank may be maximum Rs.7.50 crore and the balance of Rs.2.50 lac would be the 'Margin' money from the other Project sources.

  In case of non-funded facility by way of Deferred Payment Guarantee, the vendor of fixed assets will obtain payment direct from concerned borrower periodically as may be agreed. However, Deferred Payment Guarantee is a 'cushion' for the vendor to protect against any default by the buyer. Thus, Bank/Financial Institutions executing such Guarantee undertakes a contingent liability. In this respect, usually Bank/Financial Institutions insists for some cash margin of at least 10% of the amount of Guarantee as a cushion to protect itself from any possible claim of the vendor on default by the project borrower.

- However, 75% loan or 10% margin against Deferred Payment Guarantee is only Outer Limit. Actual amount will be subject to analysis of Balance Sheet, Profit and Loss Account, Past and Projected, Fund Flow statements, Accounting Ratios as explained earlier. Exceptions may be made where justified.

2. **Working Capital by Way of Cash Credit/Overdraft/Bill Finance, etc.:** Generally, working capital requirements for infrastructure projects are limited to Rs.5 crore in the form of cash credit/overdraft or Bill Finance. Hence, in accordance with the existing guidelines, the assessment is to be made by TURNOVER method. Accordingly, on the basis of projected sales (the factors taken into consideration for such projection be realistically examined), working capital limit be fixed at 20% of annual projected turnover. The amount so assessed may then be suitably bifurcated in consultation with the borrower into Cash Credit/Overdraft and Bill Finance.

While Bill Finance, especially Demand Documentary Bill, being self-liquidating nature is encouraged in case of various types of borrower, in reality, this type of Bill Finance does not arise in case of infrastructure projects. However, advance against receivable/book debt of the project by way of cash credit (Hypothecation) may act as a substitute for Bill Finance.

Format of Turnover Method of Computation: Applicable in any case where maximum working capital requesting is upto Rs. 5 crore.

	Component	Amount
(*A*)	Projected Business Turnover (*i.e.*, Sales/execution of jobs, etc. for next one year.	
(*B*)	25% above Turnover.	
(*C*)	5% mandatory deduction as per existing guideline on Projected Turnover (A).	
(*D*)	Maximum limit 20% of Projected Turnover (*i.e.*, B minus C).	
(*E*)	Net Working Capital (NWC) already available (*i.e.*, Current Assets minus Current Liability) of an existing unit.	
(*F*)	Amount being Higher of C (5% mandatory) or E (NWC).	
(*G*)	Permissible Limit B (25% of turnover) minus F.	

For Borrowers requesting for Working Capital Limit over Rs.5 crores: Some borrowers require higher level of working capital finance in the context of their level of operations, specific business features and above all, overall business size. In such cases, Turnover method would not be applicable. Hence, Standard Working Capital Assessment Method as under be considered:

Peak Level Holding Period	Components as may be applicable in any project	Amount
1. Days/Weeks/Months	Of: Raw Material requirement	
2. Days/Weeks/Months	Of: Consumables/Stores	
3. Days/Weeks/Months	Of: Work-in-Process (Stock-in-Process)	
4. Days/Weeks/Months	Of: Finished Goods	
5. Days/Weeks/Months	Of: Receivables (Trade Credit to customers)	
6. Day-to-day Running	Expected for: One Month	
Minus (*a*) Advance Payments from Customers. (*b*) Trade Credit available on purchases	**Total**	
Total Working Capital Requirement		

Although the above format is mainly applicable for usual manufacturing or allied business units, for each specific type of infrastructure project (depending upon its nature of service) suitable modification may be made.

3. **Non-Funded Working Capital Assistance:** At times, the borrowers are in a position to obtain funds in advance/security deposit from their buyers and/or obtain material, spare parts required for day to day use from their sellers on credit terms against Bank Guarantee. For this purpose, there is no structured method of assessment (as is available for funded working capital stated above). The usual process applied generally in such cases is as under:

   (*A*) To ascertain the maximum level of trade advances/trade credit as may be available.

   (*B*) How much margin be available from the borrower (*i.e.*, how much percentage of A above may be available to the borrower in cash/bank balance).

   (*C*) Then Guarantee may be issued for full amount (A) but margin (B) be kept earmarked/kept separately with the Bank as a cover should any invocation takes place.

Besides seeking Guarantee facilities, some borrowers may approach for issuing Letter of Credit (L/C) in favour of the supplier of materials spare parts etc. Such L/C facility may be on sight basis or usance basis, depending upon their business contracts with the suppliers. In this respect also, while there is no structured method of assessment, following aspects are important:

(*A*) Total amount of materials spare parts etc. to be available under L/C at any point of time.

(*B*) How much margin borrower in a position to provide on (A). For Sight L/C, sometimes even 10% margin may be in order while for Usance L/C, margin may be higher, say, 20%–25%.

(*C*) Bank may issue L/C for full amount as in (A), but margin (B) be kept earmarked/kept separately with the Bank as cover should Bank be called upon to retire bills under L/C at any point of time.

4 **Assessment of Requirement of Bid Bond/Performance Guarantee:** Although not very common, sometimes the borrowers may approach for:

- Bid Bond facility.
- If Bid is accepted-then Performance Guarantee facility also.

These facilities are non-funded in nature and are not to be treated as working capital or term finance.

Bid Bond becomes necessary when a borrower decides to participate in a valuable contract on the basis of Bid as per accepted commercial practice. The concerned party may stipulate that the participant must first arrange for Bid Bond from Bank, which is generally around 5% amount of Bid. Further, to ensure that the party is capable of completing the contract as per the agreed terms when Bid is accepted, a Performance Guarantee from a Bank, which may be 10%–20% of contract amount may be insisted. Thus, when Performance Guarantee is executed by a Bank, the liability for Bid Bond vanishes. Both Bid Bond and Performance Guarantee liabilities do not subsist at one point of time together.

There is no structured method of computation of allowable amount of Bid Bond/Performance Guarantee. However, Banks generally keep in mind following aspects:

(*A*) Nature of business for which Bid is to be made.

(*B*) Amount of contract under Bid.

(*C*) Whether Bid contract amount is realistic as compared with party's business level.

(*D*) Whether in the past the party could satisfactorily complete a contract obtained on Bid basis.

(*E*) Amount of cash margin to be provided to the Bank as a cover-usual minimum is generally 10% of Bid amount/Performance Guarantee facility.

PRECAUTIONS IN ASSESSMENT

Business fund requirement is a dynamic process and as such, cannot be estimated in advance with complete precision. Arithmetic/formula may be a facilitator in the process, but is not the final 'word' on assessment. Hence, 'flexibility' is the key input in the assessment mechanism. The underlying tenet is that a business unit should have an optimum dose of credit–it should neither be underdose nor overdose. Depending on the performance of an assisted unit, financial assistance may be scaled up or scaled down from time to time.

Post-disbursement follow up system should be so fine-tuned that end-use of funds is ensured at any point of time. Thus, assessment of requirement is not a mechanical process but is an 'indicative' tool which has to be supplemented on an ongoing basis by a robust credit administration system of the lending institutions.

Infrastructure financing being of a special nature with huge involvement of fund and having larger focus on credit risk aspects, the assessment has to be fine-tune from time to time based on past experiences.

MODEL APPLICATION FORM FOR FINANCIAL ASSISTANCE

Keeping all the aforesaid aspects in view, banks/financial institutions usually decide credit applications from Infrastructure sector. In this connection, a Model Application Form that may be submitted by a borrower is presented at Annexure I which may be adopted by a bank/financial institution with modifications as may be deemed fit.

❑❑❑

CHAPTER

7 Regulatory Framework

Infrastructure sector, unlike any other economic sector; in a country is different in many respects of which significant ones are the 'risk' element and 'socio-economic' implications. It is certainly the right concern of the regulatory authorities that an ideal balance must be maintained while looking to risk aspect in fund raising and at the same time mass welfare aspects attached to an infrastructure projects. Hence, within the broad contours of managing and regulating the supply of money for productive and welfare sectors and overseeing the entire monetary system, the regulatory authorities decide the coverage for infrastructure leading by Banks/Financial Institution. The basic motto in the regulatory framework and its implementation is: 'Drive slow and steady but must go on driving'. In other words, Lending liberally but with utmost caution is the bedrock in infrastructure regulatory framework.

RBI DIRECTIVE

Following prudential requirements have been prescribed for banks/financial institutions in regard to their infrastructural lending:

1. **Credit Exposure Limits:** Exposure limit means that a lending institution cannot exceed granting funded and non-funded facilities to a particular borrower or to all borrowers belonging to any identified business family group beyond a specific percentage of the concerned lending institution's Capital Fund. Usually, for any business sector (except infrastructure sector) the ceiling prescribed by RBI is as under:

   - *To a single borrower:* Maximum 15% of Capital fund of the lender.
   - *To all the borrowers belonging to a Group:* Maximum 40% of Capital fund of the lender.

   In the case of lending infrastructure sector relaxation has been made as under:

- *To a single borrower:* Additional 5% (*i.e.*, total 20%) provided the additional exposure is on account of infrastructure.
- To all the borrowers under a Group: Additional 10% (*i.e.*, belonging to a Group total 50%) provided the additional exposure is on account of infrastructure.

2. **Credit Risk Weight Percentage for Capital Adequacy under Pillar 1 of Basel Accord II:** RBI had advised prior to implementation of Basel Accord II that Banks, extending credit facilities to infrastructure sectors, could assign only 50% risk-weight (as against 100% usual) for Capital Adequacy requirements. However, Basel Accord II now provides variable risk weights depending upon credit rating of the borrower whether subjected to standardized approach or Internal-Rating based approach, the incentive earlier provided may not hold good any more.

   Above methodology may also apply to securitization of infrastructure sectors as well.
3. **Asset-Liability Management by Banks:** Main resource base of Commercial Banks is in the form of Customer Deposits (80% + of a Bank's Balance Sheet footing) which are farely of short time bound-generally maximum 5 years that, too, with Pre-payment options. But infrastructure credit exposure normally of a very long term nature thereby creating asset-liability duration mismatch. RBI's prudential requirement cautions banks to ensure proper mismatch of asset – liability on a continuing basis. Thus, is quite relevant from risk management angle since there is no capital adequacy requirement for Liquidity management.
4. **Timely and Adequate Availability of Credit:** RBI directive presides that banks/financial institutional must dispose of credit applicable in a time bound manner. Where credit facilities are sanctioned they also must ensure that the quantum is adequate for the requirements of the project. Furthermore at the post disbursement stage they must ensure the end-use of credit facilities by the borrowers.

IMPLICATIONS

RBI directives stated above carry following implications in respect of financing infrastructure sectors:

- Provision of higher credit exposure limits by additional 5% for single borrower and 10% for group borrower will enable banks/financial institutions to smoothen their credit exposure within the regulatory setting–the absolute quantum also may increase with their annual Net Profit and plough back as also enhancement of capital fund by raising resources.

- Concessional risk weight of 50% may not have any major impact-firstly, thus may have to be relooked with implementation of Basel Accord II and further Indian Banks are generally well-capitalised (approx. around 12% against international minimum of 8%–9% as for RBI guideline).
- Correction of Asset-Liability duration mismatch while focusing on increasing exposure to infrastructure sectors by banks is their real pressure and constraint. Short term funds (Customer Deposit) will definitely get deployed in long term uses.

  However, as Take-out financing route (refer to Chapter on 'Financing Infrastructure) would also be available besides the facility of 'securitisation', it may be possible to reasonably manage this aspect with limited aberration.
- Requirement of appropriate dose of credit and administration thereof on a time-bound manner both at pre-sanction stage and at post-disbursement stage would ensure uninterrupted credit flows to infrastructure sector. But in practice commercial spirit *i.e.*, return on investment criteria and a bank's resource management and major locational base may guide its credit flow to this sector.

FAIR PRACTICES CODE: RBI DIRECTIVE

RBI has designed an overall Fair Practices Code to be pursued by banks in extending credit facilities to any sector-including infrastructural sector as a measure of safe, sound and healthy credit practices across the financial system. In this respect major issues in the code touching infrastructure sectors are stated hereunder together with the background of such a Code.

Borrowing-Lending is a two way commercial transaction. Hence, any breach by any one party gives rise to the legal remedy to the other party. In institutional lending normally liability is linked to the borrower, once the lender has extended funds under an arrangement. Therefore, it is the borrower who is liable-question of lender-liability may not surface.

But, a trend a was set in mid 1980s in USA when a number of litigations were filed by borrowers making lenders liable for breach of contract. The contentions of the borrowers centered round the following for which compensations were demanded from the lenders:

- Cost for obtaining a replacement loan arising out of the failure of the existing lender to extend loan as required.
- Cost of lost business opportunities as funding was not available as required.
- Lost Profit in the business was to be compensated by the lender.

Upon analysis of various claims under Lender-Liability issues, a general consensus was drawn to the effect that:

(*i*) Lenders must treat their borrowers fairly.

(*ii*) If they fail to meet the reasonable expectations of the borrowers (within however the framework of the contract), the borrowers are entitled to file legal claims.

(*iii*) Besides the question of breach of contract, the claims may be necessitated due to any fraud perpetrated by the lender, *e.g.*, a loan agreement fraudulently induced.

Encouraged by the successes of some borrowers in USA, it was reported that in early 1990s, some attempts were initiated by a few borrowers in Indian Courts in vain.

RECENT REGULATORY INITIATIVES IN INDIA

As the Regulatory Authorities in India were being increasingly concerned over last five/six years as to the instances of indifference of some banks in meeting requirements of borrowers of various categories, a Working Group on "Lender-Liability" was constituted by Government of India. Based on the recommendations of the Group, Reserve Bank of India evolved Guidelines on FAIR PRACTICES CODE FOR LENDERS (FPC).

FPC Guidelines have been placed under Five divisions in General (some of the guidelines may not be directly applicable for infrastructure lending):

(*i*) Loan Application Form and Processing with special focus on priority/small borrowers seeking loans upto Rs. 2.00 lac (this does not apply for infrastructure sector).

(*ii*) Loan Appraisal with due diligence and stipulation of terms and conditions for loans.

(*iii*) Timely disbursement of sanctioned loans and subsequent charges in terms and conditions.

(*iv*) Post-disbursement supervision precautions.

(*v*) General aspects such as non-interference in the affairs of borrowers, non-discrimination on grounds of sex, etc.

Details of Fair Practices Code of RBI issued on 05/05/2003 on aforesaid five divisions are:

"(*i*) **Application for loans and their processing:**

(*a*) Loan application forms in respect of priority sector advances up to Rs. 2.00 lac should be comprehensive. It should include information about the fees/charges, if any, payable for processing, the amount of such fees refundable in the case of non acceptance of application, pre-payment options and any other matter which affects the interest of the borrower, so that a meaningful comparison with that of other banks can be made and informed decision can be taken by the borrower.

(*b*) Banks and financial institutions should devise a system of giving acknowledgement for receipt of all loan applications. Time frame within which loan applications up to Rs. 2.00 lac will be disposed of should also be indicated in acknowledgement of such applications.

(*c*) Banks/financial institutions should verify the loan applications within a reasonable period of time. If additional details/documents are required, they should intimate the borrowers immediately.

(*d*) In the case of small borrowers seeking loans up to Rs. 2.00 lac the lenders should convey in writing, the main reason/reasons which, in the opinion of the bank after due consideration, have led to rejection of the loan applications within stipulated time.

(*ii*) **Loan appraisal and terms/conditions:**

(*a*) Lenders should ensure that there is proper assessment of credit application by borrowers. They should not use margin and security stipulation as a substitute for due diligence on credit worthiness of the borrower.

(*b*) The lender should convey to the borrower the credit limit along with the terms and conditions thereof and keep the borrower's acceptance of these terms and conditions given with his full knowledge on record.

(*c*) Terms and conditions and other caveats governing credit facilities given by banks/financial institutions arrived at after negotiation by lending institution and the borrower should be reduced in writing and duly certified by the authorized official. A copy of the loan agreement along with a copy each of all enclosures quoted in the loan agreement should be furnished to the borrower.

(*d*) As far as possible, the loan agreement should clearly stipulate credit facilities that are solely at the discretion of lenders. These may include approval or disallowance of facilities, such as, drawings beyond the sanctioned limits, honouring cheques issued for the purpose other than specifically agreed to in the credit sanction, and disallowing drawing on a borrowal account on its classification as a non-performing asset or on account of non-compliance with the terms of sanction. It may also be specifically stated that the lender does not have an obligation to meet further requirements of the borrowers on account of growth in business etc. without proper review of credit limits.

(*e*) In the case of lending under consortium arrangement, the participating lenders should evolve procedures to complete appraisal of proposals in the time bound manner to the extent feasible, and communicate their decisions on financing or otherwise within a reasonable time.

(*iii*) **Disbursement of loans including changes in terms and conditions:** Lenders should ensure timely disbursement of loans sanctioned in conformity with the terms and conditions governing such sanction. Lenders should give notice of any change in the terms and conditions including interest rates, service charges etc. Lenders should also ensure that changes in interest rates and charges are effected only prospectively.

(*iv*) **Post disbursement supervision:**

(*a*) Post disbursement supervision by lenders, particularly in respect of loans upto Rs. 2.00 lac, should be constructive with a view to taking care of any "lender-related" genuine difficulty that the borrower may face.

(*b*) Before taking a decision to recall/accelerate payment or performance under the agreement or seeking additional securities, lenders should give notice to borrowers, as specified in the loan agreement or a reasonable period, if no such condition exits in the loan agreement.

(*c*) Lenders should release all securities on receiving payment of loan or realization of loan subject to any legitimate right or lien for any other claim lenders may have against borrowers. If such right of set off is to be exercised, borrowers shall be given notice about the same with full particulars about the remaining claims and the documents under which lenders are entitled to retain the securities till the relevant claim is settled/ paid.

(*v*) **General:**

(*a*) Lenders should restrain from interference in the affairs of the borrowers except for what is provided in the terms and conditions of the loan sanction documents (unless new information, not earlier disclosed by the borrower, has come to the notice of the lender).

(*b*) Lenders must not discriminate on grounds of sex, caste and religion in the matter of lending. However, this does not preclude lenders from participating in credit-linked schemes framed for weaker sections of the society.

(*c*) In the matter of recovery of loans, the lenders should not resort to undue harassment, *viz.*, persistently bothering the borrowers at odd hours, use of muscle power for recovery of loans, etc.

(*d*) In case of receipt of request for transfer of borrowal account, either from the borrower or from a bank / financial institution, which proposes to take-over the account, the consent or otherwise, *i.e.*, objection of the lender, if any, should be conveyed within 21 days from the date of receipt of request.

3. Fair Practices Code based on the guidelines outlined in the paragraph 2 above should be put in place in respect of all lending prospectively, but not later than 1st August 2003. Banks and financial institutions will have the freedom of drafting the Fair Practices Code, enhancing the scope of the guidelines but in no way sacrificing the spirit underlying the above guidelines. For this purpose, the Boards of banks and financial institutions should lay down a clear policy.

4. The Board of Directors should also lay down the appropriate grievance redressal mechanism within the organisation to resolve disputes arising in this regard. Such a mechanism should ensure that all disputes arising out of the decisions of lending institutions' functionaries are heard and disposed of at least at the next higher level. The Board of Directors should also provide for periodical review of the compliance of the Fair Practices Code and the functioning of the grievances redressal mechanism at various levels of controlling offices. A consolidated report of such reviews may be submitted to the Board at regular intervals, as may be prescribed by it."

It may be mentioned that Banks have been advised that keeping in view the overall FPC of RBI, they may draft suitable FPC applicable for the concerned Bank, if necessary, by "enhancing the scope" without however any dilution in any way whatsoever.

DUE DILIGENCE ON THE PART OF LENDERS

In respect of any loan proposal, it is expected that the lender will undertake due diligence not only to protect its funds and security interests, but also with a view to ensuring that the borrower is not unreasonably inconvenienced at any stage.

Generally, Due Diligence covers:

(*i*) Ensuring compliance of Know Your Customer (KYC) guideline.

(*ii*) Scrutiny of Loan Applications submitted by borrowers – wherever structured Loan Form is in use, the same should be filled up by the borrower complete in all respects supported by documents, where necessary. Lender must ensure this.

(*iii*) Obtain Market Report/Confidential Report/Confidential Report on the borrower and guarantor.

(*iv*) Appraisal by the lender must take into account:

- Reasonableness of business projections made.
- Overall viability of the business.
- Credit Rating of the borrower should be as per Bank's Loan Policy (under the guidelines of RBI, all exposures are to be rated).
- Sectoral Cost-Benefit Analysis so as to ascertain whether granting of loan will add some value to the society.
- Interview/discussion with borrower/guarantor concerning loan matter should always be recorded with the lender.
- Pre-sanction site visit and post-disbursement monitoring and follow up.
- Security documents to be executed by the borrower/guarantor must preferably be standardized. These should be stamped as per the Stamp Laws and be registered wherever necessary.

WHAT REMEDIES AVAILABLE TO THE BORROWER WHEN A LENDER HAS NOT COMPLIED WITH FPC?

It is neither expected nor it is always feasible for any borrower in India to seek legal remedy against a lender for breach of Fair Practices Code, affecting interests of the borrower. At the same time, it is necessary that the borrower will have easy and convenient method of expressing concern as to the violation of FPC by a lender. In this respect, as per RBI guidelines, the following remedies should be made available to the concerned borrowers:

- Each lending Bank must set up an appropriate grievance redressal mechanism to resolve disputes between the borrowers and Bank.
- The mechanism should be so structured that disputes relating to action/in action of a functionary in the Bank are heard and disposed of at least at next higher level, *e.g.*, if the grievance of the borrower is against a Branch Manager, the matter of resolving the same should be with next higher level, say, at Regional Manager level.
- Board of Directors should periodically:
  (*i*) Review the compliance aspects by the functionaries in the Bank.
  (*ii*) Assess how effectively grievance redressal mechanism in the Bank has been functioning and where necessary, initiate necessary corrective steps.

SOME COMMON INSTANCES OF GRIEVANCE OF BORROWERS FALLING WITHIN FPC

- Inordinate delay in disposal of loan application.
- In case of rejection of loan application, the specific reasons are not stated and often a vague statement like "the proposed business does not suit the Bank" is conveyed.
- Copy of executed loan agreement is not provided to the borrower.
- Change/modification in terms and conditions of sanction such as revision of interest rates/service charges, fees are implemented with retrospective effect and without prior intimation to the borrowers.
- Recalling of advances and/or other harassment steps are initiated without providing reasonable period to the borrower/guarantor to meet the requirement of the Bank.
- Lien/set off undertaken without appropriate prior notice to the concerned parties.
- Wherever a borrower intends to switch over from existing lending bank, the consent/rejection in the matter is inordinately delayed.

LONG TERM RESOURCE RAISING BY BANKS FOR INFRASTRUCTURE LENDING

Since financing infrastructure projects involve large sums of money and on a long term basis, in order that banks do not suffer constraint of funds and Asset-Liability duration mismatch the following window of banks' raising of resources is available.

(*i*) Issue of Long Term Debt Instruments as an aid to Capital Adequacy ratio under Basel Accord II Risk Management as also to hold sufficient funds to finance infrastructure projects. Also many banks – both in public sector as also private sector are now on the move to raise equity capital on follow on issues/private placement etc.

(*ii*) Liquidity Support from Infrastructure Development Finance Co. Ltd. (IDFC). The Government of India has promoted the Company to directly finance infrastructure projects as also to provide liquidity support to banks in their efforts to finance infrastructure sectors increasingly. In this context the gist of RBI's directive is as under:

- This finance from IDFC to the financing bank will be treated as REFINANCE.
- Where a bank may require refinance, at the point of sanction (by the bank to the borrower) it must obtain specific commitment from IDFC for reference of Principal + Interest.
- Such reference may be available after an agreed period – usually after 5 years from the date of disbursement of fund to the borrower.
- Credit risk would always remain with the financing bank/ institution and would not be transferable to IDFC.
- It would be the concerned bank's/financial institution's responsibility to repay reference amount as may agreed to with interest which may also be as per its agreement with IDFC. Such interest rate on reference may be as per Bench Mark Prime Lending Rate (BPLR) of IDFC.
- The process of obtaining refinance by a bank has another favourable side issue-appraisal skills by IDFC would be available since before committing for reference for an infrastructure loan/advance it would also undertake an assessment of the project. Thus, if a bank's approval process matches with that of IDFC then only the project would be eligible for financing to the borrower and thereafter refinancing by IDFC.

IMPLICATION OF STATE GOVERNMENT GUARANTEE FOR INFRASTRUCTURE LENDING

Since various infrastructure projects are located within states and some are Government owned entities also, it is often possible that concerned State Government may incentivise the promotion of the project by providing its Guarantee for the borrowing for the project. In this context, the gist of RBI directive is as under:

- Financing should not be done solely based on the strength of State Government Guarantee, usual Due Diligence exercise on the viability aspects of the projects must be undertaken on commercial basis by the banks/financial institutions.
- State Government's Guarantee should not be treated as a substitute for satisfactory appraisal.
- Appraisal requirements are not to be diluted under any circumstances. The "individual compacts of financing and returns on the project are well – defined on other considerations".

❑❑❑

CHAPTER

8 Terms and Conditions of Sanction and Security Documentation

Upon being satisfied of the merits of the credit application and deciding to lend upto certain limit for the facilities duly assessed, next logical step is to fix up various terms and conditions for the sanction including security documentation in conformity with laws. They may broadly be classified as under:

1. Main Terms and Conditions

- Nature of charging of security, *e.g.*, hypothecation, mortgage, etc.
- Specific documentation formalities to be carried out by the borrower/ guarantor so as to avail sanctioned facilities; this may cover submission of Board Resolution in case of limited company borrower / guarantor, formalities relating to creation of charge on securities by execution of Mortgage Deed or Memorandum of deposit of title deeds and other documents; producing NOC from concerned authorities, etc.
- Depositing cash margin where stipulated, *e.g.*, Guarantee/LC facilities, *inter alia*, with some cash margin.

2. Additional Terms and Conditions

- Execution of various Undertakings such as agreeing not to repay unsecured loan, if any, from associates without prior consent of the lenders and where to be paid not beyond a certain rate of Interest with the permission of lending institute.
- Routing all business transactions through the lenders account and where necessary opening of Escrow Account.

REASONS FOR SPELLING OUT TERMS AND CONDITIONS

Borrowing and Lending transaction is a commercial contract and as such, must be based on clear terms and conditions. In case of eventual breach of any of the terms, it will remain open for the party affected to claim damages.

In case of lending-borrowing transaction, terms and conditions play special role as under:

- Borrower acknowledges that lender may extend credit upto an agreed amount (technically known as Limit in banking), provided securities remain intact as per agreed terms and all the covenants are complied with.
- In case of secured facilities granted on Hypothecation/Mortgage basis the borrower is aware that on the default, if any, or breach of any terms and conditions, lender may deal with the securities towards repayment of the advance.
- Borrower agrees to pay interest as per terms and conditions as also fees/charges of the lender from time to time.
- The borrower agrees to keep the securities insured against usual risks and in case this is not done, the lender is empowered to do the needful at the cost, risk and responsibility of the borrower.
- When an advance is covered by Third Party Guarantee including Government Guarantee the terms and conditions of Guarantee need to be adhered to by the Guarantor and in executing the Guarantee, the Guarantor acknowledges the fact that should there be any default by the borrower, then lender may initiate action for recovery against him either singly or jointly with the borrower.

In case of secured advance, by way of Hypothecation/Mortgage obtaining of security should be backed by:

- Appropriately drafted security documents enforcing, *inter-alia*, rights to the lender in case of any breach by the borrower.
- Such documents wherever necessary are to be stamped in accordance with Stamp Act of the country.

Secured Loans and Advances may be broadly as under:

(*i*) Against pledge of securities such as Share Certificates, NSCs, etc. or even Fixed Deposit Receipt of the Bank which generally do not arise in case of infrastructure financing.

(*ii*) Hypothecation of moveable assets of the borrower such as machinery and equipments, book-debt, etc.

(*iii*) Mortgage-mostly Mortgage by Deposit of Title Deeds relating to immoveable properties of the borrower.

Security documentation for pledge advance is fairly simple and straightforward, since concerned securities such as share certificates, NSCs, etc. remain with the lender. Even for advances to a limited company, no registration of pledge charge is required.

Hypothecation of moveable assets (often described as Mortgage of Moveable) is effective only when appropriate security document is executed by the concerned party, empowering lender, *inter alia*, to take possession of hypothecated securities and dispose of the same at its discretion wherever there is any breach by the borrower. Hypothecation advances to even limited company must be registered with the Registrar of Companies within the stipulated period as per Contract Act. There is no separate format for document of Hypothecation. Each lender may have his own format. Since Infrastructure lending is generally on Consortium/Syndication basis such documents are specifically drafted by the common lawyer of the lenders.

Mortgage relates to offering charge over immoveable properties such as land, building or machinery embedded on the earth. In great majority of cases, Mortgage by Deposit of Title Deeds (S 58-f of Indian Transfer of Property Act) is stipulated, when it is agreed to offer charge over immoveable properties. Although execution of such mortgage is simple, in some States, *e.g.*, Maharashtra, for mortgage by way of Deposit of Title Deeds, appropriate stamp duty is to be paid and hence, this aspect has to be stipulated as one of the essential terms and conditions. Further, for advances to even limited company mortgage charge (whatever be the form of mortgage) is required to be registered with the Registrar of Companies under Contract Act. There is no prescribed Mortgage Deed for Mortgage by Deposit of Title Deeds. Draft for each case is prepared separately.

The modality of creation of security charging and the precautions to be taken are not the subject of this treatise. These are legal aspects and borrower/lender should obtain legal advice where considered necessary. Usually as large sums of money and lent in case of infrastructure process, all these aspects are taken care of by the concerned Lawyer.

STANDARD STRUCTURE OF SECTION TERMS AND CONDITIONS FOR LENDING TO INFRASTRUCTURE COMPANY

1. **Facility:** Term Loan
2. **Limit:** Rs...
3. **Purpose:** Developing the express highway between Tindivanam-Ulundurpet section of NH-45, located in Tamil Nadu state.
4. **Tenor of Loan:** 20 years (Three Years Moratorium *i.e.*, one year construction period and two years from Commercial Operations Date) repayable in monthly/quarters instalments.

5. **Security**

A. (*i*) First charge on all the company's immovable/movable properties (including all receivables) both present and future by way of Hypothecation/Mortgage as may be considered legally affective.

(*ii*) Assignment of all the rights, titles and interests of the company in, to and in respect of all assets of the project.

(*iii*) Assignment of insurance policies, contractor guarantees, contractor performance bonds and liquidated damages.

(*iv*) Pledge of the equity shares held by the sponsors in the company with Non-Disposal undertaking is paid-off.

The aforesaid charge will rank *pari-passu* with the charges created/to be created in favour of participating institutions/ banks (generally infrastructural financing is on Consortium/ Syndication arrangement).

Guarantee of .... State/Central Government/... Co. Ltd./ Mr./Mrs.

B. Rate of Interest: Interest @ 9.25% (Fixed) with monthly rests, with a right to reset the interest at the end of every three years keeping the current spread interest to be serviced in monthly basis.

C. All usual processing charges/fees etc. as may be stipulated by the participated Banks/Finance Institutions.

6. Working Capital Facility by way of Cash Credit/Overdraft (3) LC/Guarantee on similar basis with modification as may be necessary.

OTHER TERMS AND CONDITIONS

Stipulation of additional terms and conditions depends on case-to-case basis as may be agreed to by the borrower and lender. Some usual additional terms and conditions are as under in case of infrastructure financing.

Borrower to undertake that

- The Sponsors shall bring stipulated portion of the proposed Equity Contribution as per the Base Case Business Plan for the project upfront; such capital contribution is mentioned in the Project Report.
- Irrevocable and unconditional, undertaking that in case of events they would take steps as under:

(*i*) For any cost overrun beyond the estimated Project Cost to the extent of certain specific percentage as may be agreed to at the time of sanction.

(*ii*) To cover any shortfall in the amount payable in respect of the Facility in the event of termination on any account.

- The Borrower shall enter into a Engineering Procurement and Construction (EPC) contract on terms and conditions satisfactory to Lenders. The EPC Contractor either by itself or through its sub-contractors shall provide performance guarantees in favour of the Borrower by way of a bank guarantee from a bank acceptable to Lenders and in a form and manner acceptable to Lenders.

Condition Precedent to Signing of Financing Agreements: Signing of Financing Agreements by the Lenders shall be subject to the satisfaction or waiver in writing by the Lenders of the following Conditions Precedent to Signing of Financing Agreements:

- A copy of the Lenders Engineer's reports which shall include, amongst other things, a review of the EPC cost and Q&M costs (including preventive maintenance costs).
- The entire means of financing shall be tied up to the satisfaction of the Lenders.
- All the Project Agreements shall be executed to the satisfaction of the Lenders. Provided, however, the Substitution Agreement and Escrow Agreement shall be executed prior to first draw down.
- Borrower has obtained all necessary statutory and other approvals.
- All representations and warranties contained in the financing documents shall be true and correct in all respects.
- There shall be no existing Event of Default which has not been settled.
- A certificate preferably from a qualified Company Secretary or Chartered Accountant confirming that the borrowing under the Financing Agreements in full would not cause any borrowing limit binding on the Borrower to be exceeded.
- The Sponsors shall have contributed required portion of the Equity Contribution.
- The Borrower has provided evidence that the Borrower has finalized the insurance package and provided satisfactory evidence that the insurance policies are in full force and effect.
- The Borrower shall have paid all fees, expenses and other charges that have fallen due and are payable by it under the Financing Agreements or in connection with the Project.

Conditions Precedent to Subsequent Draw Down of Facility: Each draw down will be subjected to (without limitation) satisfaction or waiver in writing by the Lenders of the following:

- Borrower shall have performed all of its obligations under each of the Financing Agreements and Project Agreements required to be performed on or prior to such date of draw down;
- No Event of Default is outstanding or might result from the making of the relevant draw down;
- No event has occurred which has a Material Adverse Effect ("Material Adverse Effect" means the effect or consequence of any event or circumstance, which, in the reasonable opinion of the Lenders is or is likely to:
  (*i*) Be adverse to the ability of the Borrower to meet any of its financial obligations under the Financing Agreements or Project Agreements in accordance with their respective terms; or
  (*ii*) Adversely affect the legality, validity or enforceability of any of the provisions of the Financing Agreements or the Project Agreements; or
  (*iii*) Adversely affect the ability of any of the Sponsors members to perform its financial obligations under any of the Financing Agreements.
- Evidence has been provided to the Lenders that Equity Contribution, if required till that date under the Financing Agreements, to be contributed to the SPV have been duly contributed;
- All other documents, opinions, certificates, consents and allowances then required, under the Financing Agreements and the Project Agreements, in connection with that draw down have been delivered.
- Following the draw down, the Total Debt to Equity contribution ratio shall not be greater than that as may be agreed to at the time of sanction.

The Borrower shall not create or assume or incur or suffer to exist any indebtness except for:

- The Facility and such other indebtedness the Borrower may incur as per the Financing Plan approved by Lenders;
- Working capital facilities to the extent as may be approved by Lenders, if any.

Restricted Payments: The Borrower shall not:

(*i*) Pay dividends (either in cash or property) or make distributions in respect of equity; or (*ii*) Make any investment (other than a permitted investment) in any entity; or

(*iii*) Prepay or redeem for value, any indebtness of the Borrower that is subordinated to the Facility, prior to the scheduled maturity of such indebtedness (the foregoing being called "Restricted Payments").

Inspection: The Borrower shall, at its cost, permit Lenders or its authorized representatives to carry out technical, legal or financial inspections, including, but without limitation, in respect of the Project, Project facilities, works, site, buildings and books of accounts from time to time without any prior notice.

❑❑❑

CHAPTER 9 Case Studies on Infrastructure Lending

Infrastructure lending is in many ways different from any standard lending propositions such as financing capital expenditure and working capital for manufacturing/industrial segments of varying sizes and composition or for any other business sectors. This is primarily because Infrastructure lending is of long maturity duration proposition and hugely capital-asset intensive. Furthermore socio-centric dimensions such as provision of cheap utility services for the masses as is the avowed objective under a national priority list has a lot of reflections on commercial pricing of services of any infrastructure project.

In light of the above the study of each infrastructure project deserves different treatment keeping in view, however, the canons of lending and specific regulatory prescriptions wherever applicable. No straight-jacket formula or outline is possible. One common aspect in infrastructure lending is however, that it must be on secured basis covered by Hypothecation/ Mortgage/Assignment of tangible securities of the project. Unsecured (clean) lending is not encouraged. Documentation aspects are generally more comprehensive and often complicated. Hence, reputed lawyers with specialization documentation for lending should be engaged.

Looking to the prevailing thrust in specific sectors within the overall category of infrastructure projects, Two case studies on the following are presented with variations in the matter of presenting the same and drawing conclusions there from:

1. **Expressway financing**
2. **Power generation financing**

1. CASE STUDY OF ROAD PROJECT**

Sponsor Analysis: India Express Ltd. (IEL) has been promoted as a special purpose vehicle (SPV) company to implement the 53 Kms Road Project, in Tamil Nadu. IVRCL would hold 100% equity in IEL through its road investments **and Contractors** holding company *viz.*, National Road Toll Limited (NRTL).

NRTL as a class-I contractor and has over a period of last one decade emerged as one of the leading contracting companies of India.

Financial Position of NRTL

(Rs. in Crore)

Particulars	March 2006	March 2007	March 2008
Operating Income	776.59	1071.34	1521.42
EBITDA	61.53 (8%)	93.44 (9%)	140.03 (9.2%)
PBIT	50.16	82.89	129.1
Interest & Fin Charges	17.30	22.19	25.3
PAT	38.98 (5%)	57.13 (5%)	92.9 (6.1%)
Gross Fixed Assets	108.05	127.59	NA
Investments	0.45	0.25	NA
Share Capital	10.62	16.98	21.38
Net Worth	207.05	396.70	NA
Secured Loans Ratios	237.79	273.94	NA
DER	1.22	0.84	NA
Debt/EBITDA	3.86	2.93	NA
Current Ratio	2.55	1.96	NA

Shareholding Pattern (IVRCL)

Category	Sub-Category	No. of Securites Held	% Holding
Promoter's Holding	Indian Promoters	2615103	12.23
	Foreign Promoters	0	0
	Persons Acting in Concert	139985	0.65
	Sub Total	2755088	12.88
Institutional Investors	Mutual Funds and UTI	5825930	27.24
	Banks, FIs, Insurance Co.s, Central/State Govt./Non-Govt. Institutions	34543	0.16
	FIIs	8105370	37.9
	Sub Total	13965843	65.3

** Some information/data downloaded from Internet. The case study names/data are for imaginary projects and for the purpose of understanding. Any resemblance with existing projects; if found, is a matter of coincidence.

Category	Sub-Category	No. of Securites Held	% Holding
Others	Private Corporate Bodies	1466709	6.86
	Indian Public	2988367	13.97
	NRI/OCBs	116663	0.55
	Any Other	94910	0.44
	Sub-Total	4666649	21.82
	Grand Total	**21387580**	**100**

Institutional Investors constitute the biggest category of investors in IVRCL with a share of 65.3 % of Total shares.

OVERVIEW OF IEL

Management and Shareholding Pattern of IEL: IEL was incorporated by IVRCL through NRTL in 2007 with their registered office Hyderabad, Andhra Pradesh, to implement the Project. The main objects of the company are to undertake civil, mechanical, electrical works pertaining to all types of Projects, road construction and toll collection on Build Own Operate basis (BOO), Build Own Transfer (BOT) basis, Build Own Operate Transfer (BOOT) basis.

Board of Directors

Sl. No	Name
1.	Mr. B.R.Raju, Executive Director
2.	Mr. Bhag Doshi, Chief Operating Officer
3.	Mr. Vinod Kulkarni, Civil Engineer
4.	Mr. Jai Ram, Chartered Director

Shareholding Pattern: The authorized share capital of IEL is currently at Rs. 22.05 crore, which is issued, subscribed and fully paid-up.

PROJECT DTAILS

Project Structure

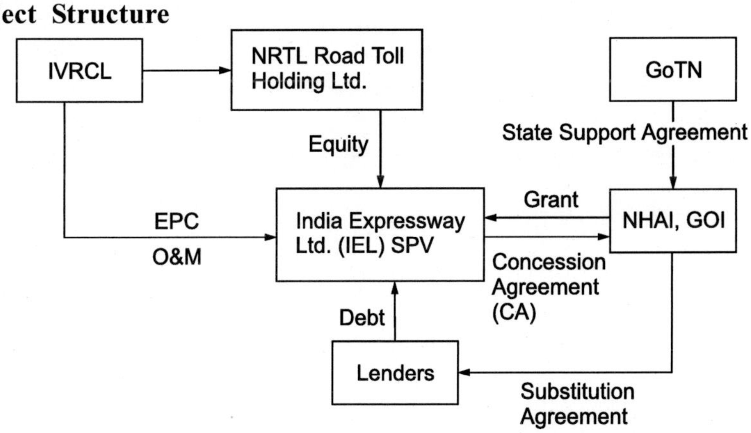

Project Description: Core Construction Requirements: Planning, design and execution of the works and other works in connection with the repair, maintenance or improvement of the Project Highway and functions associated with the construction of the Project Highway and roadside facilities. The Project Highway is to be widened to have a 4 Lane divided carriageway facility.

Service Roads: The Project includes about 33 Kms of 5.5m width Service roads at Kondalampatti, Veerapondi, Eenampiragi, Kakapalayam, Sankari, Mangarangampalayam, Palakampalayam and SSK Nagar.

Bypass Roads: The project includes about 17.5 Kms of bypass roads at Sankari, Palakampalayam and Kondalampatti.

Pavement: Pavement will be flexible for new two lanes, paved shoulders, service roads, truck lay bys, rest area, way side amenity complex and for cross roads up to 100m beyond Row limit and Rigid at Toll Plaza Location.

Intersections: There are improvements suggested for 4 four-legged intersections and 6 three-legged intersections.

Bridges and Other Structures: The Project includes construction of 12 Minor bridges including 5 new bridges, 27 slab culverts including 1 new construction, 47 pipe culverts including 9 new constructions, 1 Canal siphon/drops and 2 Flyovers at Vinayak Mission Hospital (length–75m) and Kondalampatty bypass (length–90 m) and 6 underpasses

Bid Process: IEL would have Lump sum contract with NRTL for the design, construction and development of the Project as under:

SNo	Key Term	Particulars
1.	Object	Design, Construction and Development of 53.525 Kms, 4 Lane road construction from Palem to Sukumarapalyam
2.	Type of contract	Lumpsum Turnkey (LSTK)
3.	Contractor	IVRCL Infrastructures & Projects Ltd., *NRTL*
4.	Amount	Rs.452.3 crore
5.	Way of Payment	According to attached calendar of payments (excludes advance payment). Justification of the calendar payments will be given later as an attachment to the term sheet.
6.	Delivery time	30 months
7.	Order to Proceed (OTP)	When advance payment is made
8.	LDs for delay	Back-to back with *Concession Agreement (CA)*
9.	Advance Payment	10% of EPC contract value and 5% of contract value as interest free advance against key construction equipment required.

Status of Key Approvals: A list of key approvals required for the Project and their respective status is as follows:

S.No	Approval	Approving Authority	Status
1.	Quarrying Permits	Additional District Magistrate, Erode	Applied
2.	Permission for installation of crusher	Village Panchayat and Tamil Nadu Pollution Control Board (TNPCB)	Applied
3.	Licence for explosives	Controller of Explosives	Applied
4.	Permission for installation of DG set	TNEB	Applied
5.	Permission for electrical connection	TNEB	Applied
6.	Cutting of Trees	TN Forest Department	Applied

IEL intends to enter into an O&M Agreement with NRTL for periodic maintenance every 5 years.

Environmental and Social Due Diligence: The Project shall, at all times during the currency of the assistance, comply with the environmental, health, safety and social (EHSS) requirements with provisions of all applicable legislation, and clearances issued there under, and maintenance of documents to be able to demonstrate compliance with the same.

The Company shall provide the requisite information and access to the lenders or a consultant appointed by the lenders to carry out periodic Environment & Social Monitoring and Review (ESMR) of the project and ensure compliance with specified recommendations made by lenders following the ESMR report.

Project Cost: The break up of the estimated project cost is given below:

Project Cost Item	Rs. in Crore
Engineering Procurement and Construction (EPC) cost	452.3
Preliminary and Pre-operative Expenses	7.7
Contingencies	11.3
Interest During Construction (IDC)	29.8
Total Project Cost	**501.1**

Estimated project cost and means of finance

(Rs. in Crore)

Project Cost	501.13
Financed by:	
Equity	80
Sponsors' Loan@	50
Grant from NHAI	129
Debt	292.13
-Debt A	272.13
-Debt B	20

- The Project Cost had been arrived at on the basis of estimates approved by a renowned Consultants Mr. Don Fox.
- **Letter of Acceptance by Competent GOI Authority:** Ministry of Shipping, Road Transport and Highways ("MoSRTH"), Government of India had vested with NHAI the authority to widen the existing 2 lane portion from Palem (Km 0) to Sukumarapalyam (Km 53) on NH 47 to 4 lanes through a Build, Operate and Transfer (BOT) concession.("the Project"). NHAI had accordingly invited bids in May, 2005 and after a single stage competitive bidding awarded the Project, a distance of 53 kms, on a BOT concession of 20 years to IVRCL Infrastructure & Projects Ltd., (IVRCL). Consequent to their selection by NHAI, IVRCL was issued the Letter of Acceptance.

  (Sir, I feel the Para above will give the project a basis as also connection between IVRCL and SPV would be clarified)
- The Project will be implemented over a period of 30 months after signing of Concession Agent with NHAI (National Highways Authority of India). The Concession Agreed will be operative for a period of 20 years.

MARKET ANALYSIS

The Project Road, is a section of the National Highway (NH-47) connecting Palem and Coimbatore, the two industrial cities in the state of Tamilnadu. In fact, NH-47 connects Palem and Kanyakumari through Thrissur, Cochin and Thiruvananthapuram. The entire length (53 Km) of the project road is located within Palem District. Three roads radiate from NH-47 between 29 Km. and 37 Km. One radiates towards Omalur (alternative route–SH86) and the other two towards Tiruchengodu and Erode respectively.

Sankagiri is an important town on the project road and is a market place. The Company proposed a bypass for this town.

The length of the alternate road towards Omalur is 37 km. The traffic which is destined to Karnataka or Northern Parts of India and traffic originating in Karnataka and destined to Coimbatore would divert onto this road once the toll plaza (Km 42,000) is in place. The length of Road to Omalur via Palem is 53 kms, while the alternative road is only 37 kms and therefore the alternative road is shorter by 16 kms than the project road. 100% of diversion of the north bound traffic on to this alternative road is assumed, as the alternative road is shorter by 16 kms.

Initial Traffic Level: The traffic that crosses the proposed toll plaza location at km 42,000 is estimated on the basis of a 7 day traffic count and origin destination survey at the same location by the LE-L&T Ramboll Consulting Engineers Limited (LTR).

As per the traffic surveys conducted by LTR, the present tollable traffic at Km 42,000 on the Project road for Through, Local and Monthly Pass categories has been estimated as follows:

Average Annual Daily Traffic

Key risk variable	Through	Local	Monthly Pass
Buses	198	30	762
Trucks	1862	219	120
MAV	1486	44	49
LCV	606	52	218
Cars	1367	120	222
Total Tollable Traffic in vehicles	**5519**	**465**	**1371**
Total Tollable Traffic in PCUs	**15173**	**1143**	**3416**

Traffic Growth Forecasts: Traffic growth was estimated based on elasticity method, by relating traffic growth to economic trends in influencing states. Based on traffic O-D patterns the major states of influence are Tamilnadu, Kerala and Karnataka. As per the traffic studies conducted by them, LTR has arrived at the following traffic growths for the Project road.

Vehicle Type	2006-2011	2012-2016	2017-2021	2022-2026
Bus	3.50	3.33	3.16	3.00
Trucks	6.04	5.74	5.45	5.18
MAV	7.04	6.69	6.35	6.04
LCV	6.04	5.74	5.45	5.18
Car	6.98	6.63	6.30	5.99

IDFC has also considered a uniform growth rate of 5% across the entire concession period, as another Scenario in our analysis.

Initial Tolls: Being an NHAI concession, the toll rates are linked to the increase in WPI and are subject to revision every year. The toll rates (applicable for through traffic) projected for FY 2005 based on actual WPI and FY 2009 based on 5% p.a. growth in WPI, are as follows:

Vehicle	Toll rate (Rs.)	
	FY 2005	FY 2009
Car/Jeep/Van	30	35
LCV/Mini Bus	55	65
Bus	110	130
Truck	110	130
Multi Axle Vehicle	175	205

RISK ANALYSIS

The key risks to the project are summarized in the table below.

Risk Factor	Mitigant
Traffic Risk	• Tollable Traffic had been arrived at by Independent Traffic Consultant appointed by Lenders viz., L&T Ramboll Consulting Engineers Ltd (LTR). LTR had arrived at the Tollable Traffic after conducting 7 day classified counts at 2 locations, Junction Volume Counts and Origin Destination Survey. Toll Plaza location had been identified by LTR and STL to minimize any traffic leakage on the Project Road. • Traffic Growth rates have been assumed at the rates suggested by LTR for a scenario as part of our sensitivity analysis. The Min DSCR and LLCR in that scenario are also satisfactory.
Toll Risk	• Financial indicators of the project are highly sensitive to tariff growth assumptions. Growth in tariffs is linked to the change in WPI. The base case business plan assumes that WPI would increase by 5% each year and hence, tariffs would also increase by 5% p.a. • As per the Concession Agreement, the tolls are revised every year from the 1st July based on the average of the all India WPI figures for the previous year. The WPI has increased by 5.87% p.a. between 1994-95 and 2004 and by 6.68% between 1999-2000 and 2004-05. Hence the assumption of 5% used in the business plan is reasonable.
Construction/ EPC Risk	• The Project is implemented by way of a fixed price fixed time EPC contract.

<table>
<tr><th>Risk Factor</th><th>Mitigant</th></tr>
<tr><td></td><td>• We are also stipulating a pre-disbursement condition that the terms of the EPC contract will be consistent with the requirement of CA and to the Lenders satisfaction.</td></tr>
<tr><td>Operations & Maintenance Risk</td><td>• O&M contract for periodic maintenance is likely to be awarded to IVRCL. IVRCL has substantial experience in implementing road contracts. It is also proposed to have a major Maintenance Reserve (MMR) to be built up through internal accruals from commencement of operation to cover the estimated major maintenance expenditure.
• Lenders will stipulate a condition that the terms and conditions of the O&M contractor will be to the satisfaction of Lenders and consistent with the requirements of CA.</td></tr>
<tr><td>Termination Risk</td><td>• In case of Non-Political Force Majeure, concessionaire shall receive:
— 90% of Debt Due + (sub-ordinated debt-insurance claims)
• In case of Indirect Political Force Majeure concessionaire shall receive:
— Total debt due – insurance claims + sub-debt + 110% of equity (subscribed in cash & spent on the project)
• In case of Political Force Majeure, concessionaire shall receive:
— Total Debt due +120%* Sub debt + 150%* Equity (subscribed in cash and spent on the Project)
• In case of Concessionaire Event of Default during construction period no Termination Payments are payable
• In case of Concessionaire Event of Default during operations period, concessionaire shall receive:
— 90% of Debt due – insurance claims
• In case of NHAI Event of Default, concessionaire shall receive:
— Total debt due + 120% of sub-debt + 150% of equity (subscribed in cash actually spent on project)[3]
In case NHAI fails to disburse the full termination payments within 30 days of certification by statutory auditors, then the amount remaining unpaid shall be disbursed along with interest @ SBI PLR + 2% for the period of such delay.
Hence the senior lenders are covered for up to 90 % of the amount outstanding, in all the cases of CA termination except termination under Company's EOD during construction period.</td></tr>
</table>

[2] **Source:** Economic Survey 2005

[3] if such termination occurs at any time during 3 years from Appointed date and for each successive year thereafter, such amount shall be adjusted every year to fully reflect the changes in WPI during such year and the adjusted amount arrived at shall be reduced by 7.5% pa.

Risk Factor	Mitigant
	NHAI, the Company and senior lenders will also sign a Substitution Agreement specifying the rights of step-in or substitution, available to senior lenders in case of Company's EOD. Senior lenders can substitute the Company with another person in case of the Company defaulting under CA or defaulting in making the payments to the lenders. The person substituted shall be deemed the Concessionaire under the CA.

Overall Financial Projections

(Rs. in crore)

Profit & Loss A/c	FY10	FY11	FY12	FY15	FY17	FY18	FY20	FY21
Revenues								
Traffic in PCUs	23753	24941	26188	30316	33423	35095	38692	40626
Wted Average Toll per PCU	43	45	47	55	60	63	69	73
Toll Collections	37	41	45	60	73	81	98	108
Interest on cash balance	0	0	0	0	1	1	2	3
Revenues	37	41	45	61	74	82	99	111
Expenses								
Toll Plaza Operating Expenses	3	3	4	4	5	5	6	6
Annual Maintenance Expenses	2	2	2	3	3	3	4	4
Total Operating expenses	5	5	6	7	8	8	9	10
EBIDTA	32	36	39	54	67	74	90	101
Interest	27	27	27	23	18	14	7	3
PBDT	5	9	13	31	49	60	84	99
Depreciation	29	29	29	29	29	29	29	29
Misc exp w/o	0	0	0	5	5	6	6	6
EBT	–24	–20	–16	–3	15	25	49	64
Tax	0	0	0	0	2	3	5	7
PAT	–24	–20	–16	–3	14	22	43	57

The analysis has been carried out under two scenarios.

Scenario 1: LE projected growth rate scenario

Scenario 2: Constant 5% growth rate scenario

The project provides for a pooling of the cash flows of the project along with the Sukumarapalyam–Chengapally project also being promoted by the Sponsors through the SPV–Sukumarapalyam Tollways Limited (SKTL).

As per this provision, the Company would execute a Trust and Retention Account Agreement and opened a Trust and Retention Account for pooling in the cash flows of the Project and Sukumarapalyam project being undertaken by SKTL. The pooled cash flows of both projects would be utilised for debt servicing for the Project or for the Sukumarapalyam project, at the option of the Lenders.

Sensitivity Analysis: Critical variables affecting the debt service capacity of STL are base year traffic, traffic growth rate and tariff growth rate (linked to WPI). Major maintenance cost, interest rate and routine O&M expenses are other important factors affecting the debt servicing of the Company. For each scenario, the following critical variables have been varied as part of the sensitivity analysis as below:

(*a*) Initial base traffic reduced by 10%

(*b*) Traffic growth rate reduced to 4%

(*c*) WPI growth rate which is directly linked to the toll rate growth rate is reduced from 5% to 4%.

The results of the sensitivity analysis for the combined projects basis, is set out below:

Sensitivity Analysis	Scenario 1: LE growth rates		Scenario 2: Constant 5% growth rate	
	Min DSCR	Avg DSCR	Min DSCR	Avg DSCR
Initial base traffic reduced by 10%	1.12	1.56	1.06	1.34
Traffic growth rate reduced to 4%	1.12	1.36	1.12	1.36
WPI growth rate reduced to 4%	1.20	1.56	1.11	1.34

The analysis indicates that the financial performance of the two projects together in a combined scenario is satisfactory. The minimum DSCR does not fall below 1 in any of the scenarios as seen above.

The project being a national priority and enjoys techno-economic viability, the funding as applied for is considered need based.

Hence, Banks/Financial Institutions may approve Term Loan of 272.13 crore broadly on following terms and conditions:

Interest

(*i*) The Company shall pay to the Lenders interest on the principal amount of Debt outstanding from time to time, on the last day of each calendar month in arrears (each an "Interest Payment Date"). The interest payment shall commence on the first Interest Payment Date falling after the date of first disbursement of Debt. Interest rate shall be at a rate equal to 9.25% per annum payable monthly. Interest to reset every 3 years.

Upfront Fee: The Company shall pay to Lenders non-refundable and non-adjustable up-front fee of 0.1%.

Commitment Fee: On the non-disbursed portion, as per the drawdown schedule approved by the Lenders, of Debt A, if any, the Company shall for the period from the scheduled drawdown to the actual drawdown pay to the Lenders a commitment fee at the rate of 0.5% p.a.

Repayment: The Company shall repay Debt A in 138 monthly structured instalments commencing from first date of drawal of loan.

(*a*) A first charge and mortgage of all the Company's immovable properties, present and future;

(*b*) A first charge by way of hypothecation of all the Company's movables, including movable machinery with the exception of crushers, machinery spares, tools and accessories, present and future;

(*c*) A first charge of all the book debts, operating cash flows, revenues and receivables, of the Company, present and future including by way of a charge on the Escrow Account, Retention Account, Debt Service Reserve Account and other reserves and bank accounts of the Company wherever maintained subject only to the charge of the working capital lenders;

(*d*) A first charge on the Escrow Account, Debt Service Reserve Account and other reserves and any other bank accounts of the Company, wherever maintained;

(*e*) A first charge on all intangibles of the Company including but not limited to goodwill, uncalled capital, present and future;

(*f*) A first charge by way of assignment or creation of charge of (*i*) all the right, title, interest, benefits, claims and demands whatsoever of the Company in the Project Documents (including but not limited to the Concession Agreement, the Engineering, Procurement and Construction (EPC) Contract, O&M Contract), duly acknowledged and consented to by the relevant counter-parties to such Project Documents, all as amended, varied or supplemented from time to time; (*ii*) all the rights, title, interest, benefits, claims and demands whatsoever of the Company in the Clearances relating to the Project; (*iii*) all the right title, interest, benefits, claims and demands whatsoever of the Company in any letter of credit, guarantee, performance bond provided by any party to the Project Documents and (*iv*) all Insurance Contracts/Insurance Proceeds;

(*g*) Pledge of 51% of the shares of the Company held by the Sponsors upto the third anniversary of the COD and 26% thereafter. The shares to be pledged shall be free from any restrictive covenants/

lien or other encumbrance under any contract/arrangement including shareholder agreement, joint venture agreement, financing arrangement with regard to pledge/transfer of the shares including transfer upon enforcement of the pledge.

The Security Interest set out above shall rank *pari-passu* amongst the Lenders and with the banks/financial institutions providing performance bank guarantees for the Project in terms of the Concession Agreement.

Pre-Disbursement Conditions: The obligation of Lenders to make the first disbursement shall be subject to the Company complying with the conditions given below besides compliance by the Company with the disbursement procedure stipulated by Lenders to the satisfaction of Lenders. The Company shall have:

1. Tied up the Means of Finance for the Project;
2. Confirmed that 50% of Equity has been subscribed and paid up and obtained firm commitments for the balance equity;
3. Confirmed that 50% of the Sponsor Loan has been brought in;
4. Carried out such alterations to its Memorandum and Articles of Association as may be required by Lenders (including but not limited to incorporation of clause providing for the appointment of nominee directors of banks and financial institutions on the Company's Board and transfer of shares pledged with Lenders);
5. Created the Security Interest stipulated as above;
6. Obtained all the Clearances (statutory and non-statutory) for the Project to the satisfaction of Lenders and the same shall be in full force and effect and all conditions of Clearances, if any, shall have been satisfied, except for those Clearances that are not required to be obtained or issued or such conditions of Clearances which are not required to be satisfied until a later stage of execution or operation of the Project, and Lenders shall have received copies of all such Clearances received, and all evidence for the satisfaction of the conditions of such Clearances.
7. Procured and furnished joint and several undertakings from the Sponsors that:
   (*a*) any shortfall in the resources of the Company for completing the Project and/or overrun in the cost of the Project shall be met by the Sponsors by way of equity, unsecured loans on terms and conditions acceptable to the Lender;
   (*b*) they will ensure that the Company is provided with the requisite technical, financial and managerial expertise to perform/discharge

its obligations under the Concession Agreement ("CA") to ensure that the Project is not abandoned till all the moneys of the Lenders are paid and discharged in full; and

(*c*) any overrun in the operation and maintenance ("O&M") expenses over those budgeted shall be borne by the Sponsors.

8. Entered into the EPC Contract to the satisfaction of Lenders and in compliance with the Concession Agreement;

9. Entered into the Escrow Agreement and the Substitution Agreement for the Project;

10. Shall have executed the Trust and Retention Account Agreement and opened a Trust and Retention Account for pooling in the cash flows of the Project and Sukumarapalyam project being undertaken by Sukumarapalyam Tollways Limited and agree that the said cash flows may be utilised for debt servicing for the Project or for the Sukumarapalyam project, at the option of the Lenders;

11. Appointed a reputed engineering firm/consultant as Lenders' Engineer for monitoring the implementation of the Project on behalf of Lenders and reporting the progress directly to Lenders. The Lenders' Engineer shall have submitted a report regarding the design, engineering and drawings, capital costs and maintenance costs, implementation plan and other related aspects and the Company shall have agreed to implement the recommendations of the Lenders Engineer;

12. Satisfied Lenders that all the conditions precedent to the Concession Agreement, other Financing Documents, and other Project Documents have been fulfilled by all concerned parties; and

13. The Company shall submit the following to Lenders and address concerns, if any to the satisfaction of Lenders:

- Copies of approval and clearances obtained from concerned State departments
- Health and Safety Management Plan
- Emergency Management Plan
- Environmental Management Plan (EMP) with allocation of resources, both manpower and financial, in addressing environment pollution (air, water, solid waste and noise), health, safety and social concerns of the project. The EMP shall deal with aspects, including but not limited to the following ones:
  - — Management plan for affected water bodies along the Project.
  - — Ensuring compliance with conditions/provisions of various consents/clearances/approvals obtained for the Project during both construction and operation.

Projected Profit & Loss A/c

Rs. Crore

Profit & Loss A/c Revenues	FY10	FY11	FY12	FY13	FY14	FY15	FY16	FY17	FY18	FY19	FY20	FY21	FY22
Traffic in PCUs	23753	24941	26188	27497	28872	30316	31832	33423	35095	36849	38692	40626	42658
Toll Collections-Through Traffic	30	33	36	40	44	49	54	59	65	72	79	88	97
Toll Collections-Local Traffic	0	0	1	1	1	1	1	1	1	1	1	1	1
Toll Collections-MP Traffic	7	7	8	9	10	11	12	13	14	16	18	19	21
Wted Average Toll per PCU	43	45	47	50	52	55	57	60	63	66	69	73	77
Toll Collections	37	41	45	50	55	60	67	73	81	89	98	108	120
Interest on cash balance	0	0	0	0	0	0	1	1	1	1	2	3	4
Revenues	37	41	45	50	55	61	67	74	82	90	99	111	
Expenses													
Toll Plaza Operating Expenses	3	3	4	4	4	4	4	5	5	5	6	6	6
Annual Maintenance Expenses	2	2	2	2	3	3	3	3	3	3	4	4	4
Total Operating expenses	5	5	6	6	6	7	7	8	8	9	9	10	10
EBIDTA	32	36	39	44	48	54	60	67	74	81	90	101	114
Interest	27	27	27	26	25	23	21	18	14	10	7	3	0
PBDT	5	9	13	18	23	31	39	49	60	71	84	99	113
Depreciation	29	29	29	29	29	29	29	29	29	29	29	29	29
Misc exp w/o	0	0	0	5	5	5	5	5	6	6	6	6	6
EBT	–24	–20	–16	–15	–10	–3	6	15	25	36	49	64	78
Tax	0	0	0	0	0	0	1	2	3	4	5	7	9
PAT	–24	–20	–16	–15	–10	–3	5	14	22	32	43	57	69

Projected Cash Flows

Rs. Crore

Cash Flow Statement	FY10	FY11	FY12	FY13	FY14	FY15	FY16	FY17	FY18	FY19	FY20	FY21	FY22
Chash Inflows EBIDTA	32.4	35.7	39.4	44.1	48	54	60	67	74	81	90	101	114
Drawals from MMRA	0	0	0	0	0	0	0	0	19	0	0	0	0
Inflows from DSRA	0	0	0	0	0	0	0	0	0	1	0	1	10
Cash shortfall loan from promoter				4									
Cash Inflows	**32**	**36**	**39**	**48**	**48**	**54**	**60**	**67**	**93**	**82**	**91**	**103**	**124**
Cash Outflows													
Tax	0	0	0	0	0	0	1	2	3	4	5	7	9
Interest	27	27	27	26	25	23	21	18	14	10	7	3	0
Principal Repayment	1	3	6	11	14	20	28	37	40	40	43	42	2
Major Maintenance Expenses	0	0	0	24	0	0	0	0	32	0	0	0	0
Additions to MMRA	0	0	0	0	0	0	6	6	6	8	8	8	8
Outflows to DSRA	0	0	0	0	0	0	7	6	0	0	0	0	0
Cash Outflows	29	30	33	61	39	43	63	69	95	63	64	60	20
Cash and Bank													
Opening Balance	0	4	9	16	3	12	23	20	18	16	34	61	104
Net Cash Flows	4	`6	7	–13	9	11	–3	–3	–2	19	27	42	104
Closing Balance	4	9	16	3	12	23	20	18	16	34	61	104	208

Projected Balance Sheet

Rs. Crore

Balance Sheet	FY10	FY11	FY12	FY13	FY14	FY15	FY16	FY17	FY18	FY19	FY20	FY21	FY22
Sources of Funds Equity	80	80	80	80	80	80	80	80	80	80	80	80	80
Promoters Loan	0	0	0	4	4	4	4	4	4	4	4	4	4
Retained Earnings	–38	–58	–74	–89	–99	–102	–96	–83	–61	–29	15	71	141
Grant	129	129	129	129	129	129	129	129	129	129	129	129	129
Senior Debt	271	268	263	252	238	219	192	156	118	80	39	0	0
Subordinated Debt	20	20	19	19	18	17	16	14	12	10	7	5	3
Total Sources	**462**	**439**	**417**	**394**	**370**	**348**	**325**	**301**	**283**	**274**	**274**	**289**	**356**
Application of Funds													
Net Fixed Assets	458	430	401	372	344	315	286	258	229	200	172	143	115
Cash and Bank	4	9	16	3	12	23	20	18	16	34	61	104	208
MMRA	0	0	0	0	0	0	6	13	0	8	17	25	34
DSRA	0	0	0	0	0	0	7	13	13	12	12	10	0
Misc exp not w/o	0	0	0	19	14	9	5	0	25	19	13	6	0
Total Application of Funds	**462**	**439**	**417**	**394**	**370**	**348**	**325**	**301**	**283**	**274**	**274**	**289**	**356**

2. CASE STUDY ON POWER GENERATION PROJECT**

Project Brief: ABC Power Private Limited (APPL), a company promoted by ABC Group, is setting up a 600 MW (2 × 300 MW) coal based power plant in the Munada Special Economic Zone (MSEZ) located in the Munadah District of Gujarat.

The power project is proposed to be implemented by way of different packages including for Turnkey Supply, Erection, Commissioning and Testing etc. The company would be assisted by engineering consultants/ competent professionals in formulating the concepts, systems, basic and detailed engineering, procurement, construction management services, erection and testing management services, inspection and quality control.

In this regard, XYZ Consulting Engineers (India) Pvt. Ltd. (XYZ) has been appointed by the company as the **Owners' Engineer** for the preparation of the bid documents and finalization of the contracts. Further, the company proposes to undertake the operations and maintenance of the project in-house.

The primary fuel for the power project is imported coal. The company proposes to procure its entire imported coal requirement, which is estimated at 1.8 MTPA, from the ABC Group companies. It may be mentioned that AEL is a leading player in the country for import of coal and is projected to import about 8.0 million tonnes (MT) of coal in Financial Year (FY) 2006 which would constitute about 60% of the projected total coal imports in India in FY 2006 and used for power generation.

Further, the coal would be imported via Munada port, which is at a distance of about 25 kilometers (kms) from the project site and thereafter transported to project site by rail through a dedicated railway line, which is being developed as a part of the project.

The entire power generated by the power plant would be sold to the Gujarat state utility/the electricity trading company of the ABC Group/ SEZ. The tariff applicable for the state utility has been computed as per the guidelines stipulated by Central Electricity Regulatory Commission (CERC). The entire power shall be evacuated through a twelve (12) kms long double circuit 220 kilo Volt (kV) transmission line, which is being implemented as a part of the project.

** Some information/data downloaded from Internet. The case study names/data are for imaginary projects and for the purpose of understanding. Any resemblance with existing projects; if found, is a matter of coincidence.

COST OF PROJECT AND MEANS OF FINANCING

Cost of Project: The break up of the project cost estimates is as follows:

Particulars	(Rs. million)
Land and site development	750.0
Civil works and infrastructure	2950.0
Plant & machinery	12920.3
Railway line	440.0
Preliminary & preoperative expenses	1754.4
Financing costs	1914.5
Contingency provisions	1470.8
Total Capital Cost	22200.0
Margin money for working capital	600.0
Total Project Cost	22800.0

➢ **Cost Head details:** Land & Site Development (Rs. 750.0 million)

- ✓ The company proposes to obtain 80.0 ha of land from the existing land of Munada SEZ by way of long term lease. The cost for acquiring the total land is estimated at Rs. 250.0 million. Further, an amount of Rs. 500.0 million would be incurred on the preliminary investigation and site development.

Civil Works and Infrastructure (Rs. 2950.0 million)

- ✓ The civil works and infrastructure includes development of around 5-6 independent systems such as cooling water system (Rs. 300.0 million), cooling towers (Rs. 300.0 million), township (Rs. 500.0 million) and main plant building (Rs. 1715.1 million) etc. The cost estimates are based on the prevailing rates for civil and structural work at Munada.

Plant and machinery (Rs. 12920.3 million)

- ✓ The complete plant and machinery is proposed to be procured through various contract packages. The cost estimates are based on quotations/the prevailing rates for plant and machinery. The broad items comprising the total plant and machinery for the project include (i) steam generator island (Rs. 4778.0 million); (ii) turbine generator island (Rs. 3185.0 million); (iii) cooling water system (Rs. 143.7 million); (iv) DM water system (Rs. 381.8 million); (v) coal handling system (Rs. 892.6 million); (vi) other BoP mechanical (Rs. 811.9 million); (vii) control and instrumentation (Rs. 456.1 million); (viii) LT switch-gear (Rs. 255.2 million);

(ix) transmission line (Rs. 600.0 million based on estimates); (x) 220 kV switchyard (Rs. 341.3 million); (xi) transformers (Rs. 306.9 million); and (xii) initial spares (Rs. 300.0 million).

Preliminary and Pre-operative expenses (Rs. 1754.4 million)

✓ Preliminary expenses include establishment expenses (Rs. 100.0 million), design and engineering (Rs. 90.0 million), audit and accounts (Rs. 137.2 million). Pre-operative expenses include erection testing and commissioning (Rs. 1009.6 million), start-up fuel (Rs. 100.3 million), site supervision (Rs. 119.4 million), operators training (Rs. 5.5 million) and insurance (Rs. 192.4 million).

Financing cost (Rs. 1914.5 million)

✓ Financing costs include interest during construction, up-front fees etc.

Contingency provisions (Rs. 1470.8 million)

✓ Provision for contingency has been provided at about 7.8% of all costs (excluding financing costs and margin money for working capital).

Margin Money for Working Capital (Rs. 600.0 million)

✓ Provision for margin money for working capital has been made at Rs. 600.0 million. For the purpose of the estimates, the current assets comprising of receivables of 60 days, fuel stock of 60 days, O&M expenses of 30 days and spares requirement equal to 1.0% of the capital cost has been considered.

Assessment of Project Cost

✓ The total project cost of Rs. 22800.0 million is computed on the estimates based on past experiences, consultants' recommendations, prevailing rates etc. The company is also in discussions with various agencies for the award of contracts for the implementation of the project.

MEANS OF FINANCE

The proposed means of financing for the project is as follows:

Particulars	(Rs. million)
Equity Capital	5700.0
Rupee Term Loans from FIs/banks	17100.0
Total	22800.0

The project is proposed to be financed with a debt equity ratio of 75:25 which is permissible.

Equity

✓ The entire equity capital of Rs. 5700.0 million would be brought in by ABC Group/other investors. Of the total equity of Rs. 5700.0 million, Rs. 2000.0 million would be brought in prior to disbursements. Further, ABC Group would provide an acceptable credit support for the balance equity requirement of Rs. 3700.0 million and for meeting any cost overrun.

Rupee Term Loan

✓ The total debt requirement of Rs. 17100.0 million would be tied up with domestic banks/financial institutions.

MANAGEMENT, ORGANISATION AND SHAREHOLDING PATTERN

➢ The Memorandum and Articles of Association of the company provide for a minimum of 2 and a maximum of 12 directors. The Board of APPL presently comprises 5 directors, *viz.*,

Name of Director	Representation (Promoter/Independent/Nominee)
	Director (Promoter)
	Director
	Director
	Director
	Director

Organisation

✓ Shri ..., who is assisted by the following team members, is looking after the day-to-day operations of the company:

- Shri ... , Sr. Vice-President (Power): Shri ... has about 31 years of experience in the setting up and operation of large projects.
- Shri ..., Financial Controller: Shri ... is a chartered accountant having 35 years of experience in the industry.
- Shri ..., Group President (HR): Shri ... has about 32 years of experience in Human Resource Development, Organisation Development and Corporate Communication.
- Shri ..., General Manager (Legal): Shri ... is a Masters in Business Law and has about 20 years of experience in Civil and Business laws.

Shareholding Pattern

✓ APPL currently has an authorized capital of Rs. 10.0 million of which Rs. 9.5 million is issued and paid-up by the promoters. A suitable condition has been stipulated that the authorised capital shall be enhanced in accordance with the financing plan.

DETAILS OF THE PROJECT

Location

- ✓ The project site is located in village Wandh in the Munadah district of Gujarat. The village is approachable by road NH-8A extension between Gandhidham and Mandvi towns. Further, an approach road about 15 kms long would be constructed to connect with the site. With this, the plant site would be connected by road to Munada port, which is at a distance of about 35 kms from the site. The nearest rail link available is the rail link between Munada port and Adipur station. The nearest station is Adipur/Gandhidham which is at a distance of 63 kms from the plant site. The nearest airport is Bhuj, which is at a distance of about 65 kms from the site.
- ✓ The project is proposed to be located inside the Munada Special Economic Zone (MSEZ) area, which is located at a distance of 25 kilometer (km) from Munada town. As may be noted, the site location has been selected considering the proximity of the site to Munada port and the advantages in respect of coal transportation logistics that can be leveraged. Further, the benefits of site location also include the proximity to the source of sea water (for which a channel of about 3 kms would need to be constructed), which would be required for both consumptive and cooling purposes.

Land

- ✓ The land required for the project is estimated at about 80.0 hectares. The proposed land forms a part of the land acquired by Munada SEZ and would be leased to APPL. The land is un-inhabited and no Rehabilitation and Resettlement (R&R) issues are envisaged.

Power Generation/Distribution Process

- ✓ The process of generation of power from coal (water steam cycle) essentially entails two main stages. In the first stage, the energy stored in coal is converted into heat energy in the coal-fired boilers. In the second stage, the high-pressure steam, which is generated in the boilers, is passed through turbines (conversion of heat energy into mechanical energy) which in turn is coupled to generators (conversion of mechanical energy into electrical energy), thereby generating electricity.
- ✓ The water steam cycle essentially contains the coal fired steam generator, the steam turbine with condenser, feed-water tank, Low Pressure (LP) heaters and High Pressure (HP) heaters and the connecting pipelines. The superheated steam produced in the steam generator is supplied to the steam turbine, which drives the

three-phase AC generator. After leaving the HP turbine, the steam is reheated in the steam generator and fed to the Intermediate Pressure (IP) turbine. In the LP turbine the steam coming directly from the IP turbine expands to condenser pressure and is condensed in the condenser. Closed cycle water system is used for cooling of the condenser. The condensate collected in the condenser hot well is discharged by the condensate pumps and supplied via the LP condensate heaters into the feed-water tank. The feed-water pumps discharge feed water from the feed-water tank via the HP heaters to the steam generator.

✓ The power station has been designed with two power generating units of 300 MW each, with the auxiliaries and common utility services like plant water system, coal handling system, ash handling plant, switchyard for power evacuation, plant electrical system and workshop. The main sections of the power generating unit include boiler along with milling system and electrostatic precipitator, coal handling system, turbine generator unit, boiler feed pump, condensate extraction pump, circulating and auxiliary cooling water pumps and the generator transformer with bus duct. The main sections of the utility system are the coal handling system, ash handling system, switchyard and the plant water system. The main generating equipment for the proposed project will consist of 2 nos. of Steam Turbine Generator (STG) and 2 nos. of Pulverized Coal Fired Boilers (PCFB). The power will be generated at 16.5 KV and will be stepped up to 220 KV and will be connected to the proposed 220 KV switchyard of the company for dispatch.

Plant and machinery: The main parameters of equipment for the proposed project are as indicated below:

Steam pressure at superheater inlet	150 bar
Generator Power Factor	0.85
Turbine maximum continuous rating	330 MW
Turbine RPM	3000

The key features of the main components of the plant are as follows:

Steam Turbine and Accessories

✓ The steam turbine would be 3000 revolutions per minute (rpm), tandem compound, single reheat, regenerative, condensing, horizontally split, three-cylinder machine with six (6) uncontrolled extractions for regenerative feed heating. The turbine would be designed for main steam parameters of 150 kg/cm^2 (abs) at 537-540 °C before emergency stop valves of HP turbine and reheat steam parameters of about 36 kg/cm^2 (abs) and 537-540°C at inlet to IP turbine. The LP turbine will exhaust against a condenser pressure of 0.087 kg/cm^2. At turbine valve wide open condition the turbo-generator set will be able to operate continuously.

Condensing Equipment

✓ Double pass surface condenser capable of maintaining the required vacuum while condensing steam at maximum rating of the turbine would be provided. The condenser arrangement would be such that on-load maintenance of one half of the condenser at a time is possible by isolating the same from cooling water inlet and outlet sides.

Steam Generator

✓ The steam generators which would be designed for firing 100% washed coal/imported coal and would be radiant, reheat, natural circulation, single drum, balanced draft, outdoor type of unit rated to deliver about 923 tonnes per hour (tph) of superheated steam at 174 Kg/cm^2 (abs), 540 °C when supplied with feed water at a temperature of 250 °C at the economizer inlet.

Coal Handling System

✓ The coal handling system would in normal conditions be operational for two shifts a day with provision for third shift operation. It is proposed to have sixteen (16) hours storage capacity in the bunkers. Coal from the stockyard at site would be reclaimed by a stacker-cum-reclaimer and fed to the trunk conveyor. Coal would then be fed to the power house through crushers, screens and conveyors according to the requirement of the boilers.

Cooling Water System

✓ Seawater cooling is proposed for the cooling water system. As the site is located about 3 km away to the water source, the preferred option is a closed cycle cooling system with seawater makeup. The cooling water system would comprise induced draft cooling tower, circulating water pumps and cooling water piping. Evaporative cooling tower using sea water, due to presence of dissolved salts acting as vapour pressure depressant, necessitate lower cycle of concentration, and selection of appropriate materials of construction.

Effluent Disposal System

✓ The oil sewer will collect water from the areas where there are possibilities of contamination by oil (fuel oil storage area) and the drains from such areas will be connected to an oil separator. From the oil separator the clear waste water will be led to a neutralising pit, while the oily waste sludge will be collected separately and disposed. The clarifier sludge from the pre-treatment plant clarifier in the desalination plant which is intermittent will be pumped to the sludge handling system with sludge drying bed.

Implications of Various Contracts: The Infrastructure Projects particularly power projects are contracts driven. Major contracts are as under:

(*A*) Procurement Contracts and Project Management

- ✓ The project is proposed to be implemented by way of package contracts. In this regard, the company proposes to enter into various contracts, which would be awarded to different contractors.
- ✓ The Boiler and Turbine Generator (BTG) package comprises around 40% of the total project cost. For procurement of the BTG package, the company proposes to undertake international competitive bidding and has already invited bids from international equipment suppliers. The company proposes to finalize the contractor for the BTG works by April 2006. The other independent packages are proposed to be finalized by May, 2006. It may be mentioned that the company shall be assisted in formulating the concepts, systems, basic and detailed engineering, procurement, construction management services, erection and testing management services, inspection, quality control, expediting, project management by XYZ Consultants who would be acting as the owners' consultant.

(*B*) Operation and Maintenance (O&M)

- ✓ The operations and maintenance (O&M) of the power plant would be undertaken by the company in-house. The company is also exploring the possibility of availing the services of a reputed O&M contractor. The O&M structure for the project would be decided only after the finalization of the BTG supplier and requisite arrangements would be entered prior to the commissioning of the project.

(*C*) Water

- ✓ The amount of water required for the project is estimated at about 6600 m^3/hr. The project would utilise sea water to meet both its consumptive and cooling water requirement. The proposed plant site is located 3 km from the nearest sea shore *i.e.*, Kotdi creek and the interspersed land in-between site and the sea shore is basically mud flats and sand dunes. The seawater will be drawn through the pump over an intake sump located at end of the sea water canal.

✓ The intake pump house will be provided with bar/trash screen and travelling water screen (TWS). Stop log gates will be provided for isolation. To prevent the blocking of openings of TWS by debris of sea water, 2 × 100% screen wash pump, tapping the water from the intake pump discharge header and re-circulating the same on the screen for back washing to make the system efficient has been considered.

(*D*) Coal

✓ The fuel for the power plant would primarily be imported coal. The company proposes to enter into arrangements for supply of imported coal with ABC Group companies. The total requirement of imported coal is estimated at 1.8 million tonnes per annum (MTPA) for the operation of 600 MW, considering a calorific value of imported coal of 6000 kcal/kg and the plant operating at 85% plant load factor. It may be mentioned that, the flagship company of ABC Group, *viz.*, ABC Exports Limited (AEL), is a recognized five star export house and is one of the largest importers of coal in India. While during FY 2005, AEL imported about 4.0 million tonnes (MT) of coal it is projected to import about 8.0 MT of coal in FY 2006, which would constitute about 60% of the projected total coal imports in India in FY 2006 and used for power generation. ABC Group proposes to import coal for the power plant from various countries including Indonesia, South Africa, China and Australia. Further, the ABC Group is also exploring the possibility of acquiring coal mines in Indonesia for which discussions are in an advanced stage. The company proposes to enter into long term fuel supply agreement with ABC Group for the purchase of coal. The price of coal would be fixed for a period of five years.

(*E*) Coal Transportation

✓ Coal is transported by sea in three major categories of bulk carriers *viz.*, Handymax (about 50,000 Dead Weight Tons-DWT), Panamax (about 70,000 DWT) or Cape size vessels (about 170,000 DWT). The freight for the vessels for a particular distance is determined in terms of the daily rentals and the operational cost (determined by distance) and the same varies according to the vessels. The rentals for the vessels can be benchmarked to the various indices published for type of vessel.

✓ As may be noted, the freight charges movement has been in accordance with the Baltic index movement. The freight charges have increased significantly in the year 2004 primarily due to lack of adequate shipping capacity to meet the increasing demand. However, as per industry sources, the capacities have increased in the recent past and there is a downward trend in the freight charges. As indicated in the graph, the average freight rates for the Panamax vessel for a distance of 9500 nautical miles have been about USD 25 per tonne. The per tonne charges for the capsize vessels are slightly lower due to higher capacity. Further, the above-mentioned freight chart is based on the spot rates/short-term rates. The freight charges (rental portion) are substantially lower for the long-term contracts.

✓ *A condition has to be stipulated that APPL shall finalise fuel supply agreement in a manner such that the delivered price of coal at Munada Port is fixed at USD 45.0 per tonne.*

Coal Inland Transportation Logistics

✓ Coal would be transported from the port to the plant site by a dedicated railway line of 25 kms, which is proposed to be constructed by the company at an estimated cost of Rs. 440.0 million. The cost of the railway line has been included as a part of the project cost. Two rakes with bottom opening type of wagons (approximately 50 in number for each rake) will be employed for coal transportation and these wagons will be owned by GAPL. Also, apart from the existing NH 8 A extension and SH 6, Munada SEZ is planning to build a coastal road of about 25 kms, connecting the port to plant site, parallel to railway corridor, which would provide an alternate to the transportation of coal by railways. Apart from this, facilities for unloading, weighing and storage would be established at plant site. Storage capacity of stockpile is envisaged at two-ship loads coal (for Indian and imported coal having 65,000 tonnes of capacity each) which would be equivalent to the coal requirement of about 24 days in case of imported coal and 16 days in relation to domestic coal.

Secondary Fuel

✓ Secondary fuel in the form of LDO/HFO would be required primarily for start up operations. The annual requirement of secondary fuel–LDO/HFO is estimated at 12,000 tonnes per annum. Further, secondary fuel shall be sourced from the nearest depot of Indian Oil Corporation.

Evacuation of Power

✓ The power from proposed project would be generated at 16.5 kilo Volts (kV) and will be stepped upto 220 kV and connected to the

220 kV switchyard at the project site. This would in turn be connected to the state grid through Nanikhakhar sub-station. The power is proposed to be evacuated using a double circuit 220 kV transmission line (12–14 kms) and the company proposes to setup the transmission lines as a part of the project. Two of these lines would connect the power plant to the 220 kV Nanikhakhar sub station. Additionally, the power generated is proposed to be transmitted to the SEZ in Munada through the other double circuit 220 kV transmission line connected to the Tappar substation near Varsana. The company is also exploring the possibility of connecting the project to the PGCIL grid for which discussions have already been initiated.

Schedule of Implementation

✓ The first unit of 300 MW is expected to be completed within 33 months from financial closure and the second unit of 300 MW is expected to be completed within 35 months. APPL proposes to issue the Notice to Proceed (NTP) to the BTG suppliers by the end of March 2006. It may be noted that financial closure is yet to be achieved and the date of completion of the project would be finalized at the time of financial closure. The overall time schedule for implementation of the project is as follows:

Particulars	Start	Completion
1. Financial Closure	Day 0	
Civil Works	Day 0	Day 0 + 21 months
Technical & Engineering	Day 1	Day 0 + 14 months
Delivery of BTG	**2.** Day 0 + 4 months	**3.** Day 0 + 18 months
Installation of Equipment	Day 0 + 10 months	Day 0 + 25 months
Unit I Trial Runs	Day 0 + 31 months	Day 0 + 32 months
4. Unit II Trial Runs	Day 0 + 32 months	Day 0 + 35 months
Commercial Production (Unit I)	Day 0 + 33 months	
Commercial Production (Unit II)	Day 0 + 35 months	
Total Implementation Period	35 months	

Lenders' Engineer

✓ With a view to obtain an independent opinion on the project, it is proposed to appoint Lenders' Engineer (LE) to act on behalf of the Lenders to the project. The scope of services of LE would inter-alia include – review of conceptual design including engineering, construction plans and operation plans; assessment of the investment costs; review of selection of equipment suppliers; assessment of coal supply chain; review of design parameters including output, availability and efficiency; power evacuation arrangements, water availability and adequacy of arrangements, other infrastructure availability and adequacy, assessment of operation and maintenance arrangements including provision of penalties and bonuses; verification/ support of financial model inputs; review of environmental issue, adherence; review of construction schedule, monitoring etc. The company will be required to abide by the recommendation of the Lenders' Engineer and take suitable remedial/corrective measures for which suitable condition has been stipulated.

MARKET AND SELLING ARRANGEMENTS

The Indian electricity sector has grown manifold since 1947 and India today is the third largest producer of power in Asia. The power generating capacity has increased from 1,362 MW in 1947 to about 123,543 MW as on November 30, 2005. Out of the total installed generation capacity, 57.0% is owned by the state sector, 32.3% is owned by the central sector and the balance 10.7% by the private sector. The break up of installed capacity as on November 30, 2005 is as follows:

(MW)

Source/Ownership	Central	State	Private	Total
Coal/lignite	26007	37943	4358	68308
Gas/liquid fuel	4419	3478	4532	12429
Diesel	—	477	725	1202
Hydro	6172	25054	909	32135
Nuclear	3310	—	—	3310
Renewable Energy Resources	—	3496	2663	6159
Total	39908	70448	13187	123543

As may be observed from the above, thermal power based power plants account for about 66.3% of the country's installed capacity for power generation, with coal/lignite constituting about 55% of total installed capacity. The annual per capita consumption of electricity in India is one of the lowest in the world and is estimated at about 592 units. India's per capita consumption for electricity is about one fourth of the world's average of 2373 units.

Inspite of significant increase in the installed capacity, most of the regions in the country are facing power shortages. The problem of shortage in supply becomes more acute during peak hours leading to load shedding by many utilities to maintain the grid in a healthy state. The all India average shortages for the year 2005-06, till September 2005 were 7.4% in terms of energy and 12.2% in terms of peak load.

The main reasons for the shortages in energy requirement and peak demand, are high growth in demand of power outstripping the growth in capacity addition, low Plant Load Factor (PLF) of thermal generating units in State sector and not so satisfactory record of capacity addition against the target set in IXth and Xth Plan by the Government of India.

Operational performance: AT&C losses in the state are given below:

Year	AT&C loss (%)
2000-01	28.14
2001-02	20.25
2002-03	28.75
2003-04	32.36

FINANCIALS/PROFITABILITY

(Rs. in millions)

Financial Year ending March 31	2010	2012	2015	2017	2021
No. of months of operations	12	12	12	12	12
Gross Capacity (MW)	600.0	600.0	600.0	600.0	600.0
Net Saleable Energy (MUs)	3826.4	3826.4	3826.4	3826.4	3826.4
Weighted average tariff (Rs./unit)	2.21	2.38	2.45	2.51	2.47
Total operating income (TOI)	8469.5	9123.5	9385.8	9589.8	9461.5
PBIDT	3632.1	3992.7	3846.8	3756.3	2978.5
Depreciation	1083.4	1083.4	1083.4	1083.4	1083.4
Interest	1514.2	1272.2	894.0	642.4	166.3
PBT	3632.1	3992.7	3846.8	3756.3	2978.5
PAT	1034.5	1637.1	1869.5	2030.6	1728.9
Gross cash accruals	2030.9	2582.7	2795.5	2943.1	2666.7
Net Fixed assets	19375.0	17208.2	13958.2	11791.4	7458.0
Tangible net worth (TNW)	6917.5	9847.5	14768.9	18413.9	26034.5
Long term debt (LTD)	15934.1	12825.0	8161.3	5052.2	0.0
Working capital	1642.6	1753.4	1833.2	1892.5	1950.8
Total Debt/TNW	2.54	1.48	0.68	0.38	0.07
DSCR	1.34	1.38	1.54	1.68	6.78
Average DSCR	1.65				
Min. DSCR	1.34				

STATUS OF APPROVALS

Approval/Consent	Agency	Status
Land Usage	Local Authority	In Process
Pollution Control	GPCB	In Process
Stack Height Clearance	AAI	In Process
Water Availability	GMB	In Process
Environment Clearance	GoG/MoEF	In Process
Forest clearance	MoEF	In Process

The project being a national priority and enjoys techno-economic viability, the funding as applied for is considered need based.

Hence, Banks/Financial Institutions may approved Term Loan of Rs. 1710 crore on usual terms and conditions as applicable for infrastructure lending.

This case study is focused on specific issues on Power generator. Terms and conditions aspect may be broadly same as of Case Study No.1– hence not elaborated.

3. A RECENT LARGE CASE OF AN INFRASTRUCTURE PROJECT IN INDIA

A massive Infrastructure Project is on way in Mumbai/Navi Mumbai for Construction of 22 Km Sewri Sea Link–one of the largest Infrastructure Projects has since been approved.

Main aspects of the project are as under:

- A Trans-Ocean Six lane bridge of 22 Km will connect Sewri to Nhava Sheva by Sea Link.
- Estimated Cost of Project Rs.6,000 crore to be arranged by an identified consortium.
- Project is expected to be completed to the year 2013.
- Maharashtra State Road Development Corporation will be the Nodal Agency.
- Consortium will take up the project a Design Build, Own, Operate and Transfer (DBOOT) basis.
- They will recover the cost from the revenue and will handover the project to Nodal Agency in 9 years and 11 months.

In the context of the above the relative portion of the report appearing in a renowned Newspaper is reproduced below:

"One of the world's longest trans-oceanic bridges, Sewri-Nhava Sheva link with an estimated project cost of Rs.6,000 crore was finally bagged by a consortium. Now the task of the consortium is to complete the 22 km, six-lane bridge by 2013 on Design, Build, Own, Operate and basis. However, transport and infrastructure experts believe that it will be a mammoth task to recover the costs as it will be a massive engineering and financial challenge to complete the project on time. Experts say most infrastructure projects in the city have suffered due to charges escalating beyond the total project cost.

The consortium has offered to build the 22 Km six-lane bridge, connecting Sewri to Nhava Sheva by sea link, by 2013, recover the costs from revenues and hand it back to the nodal agency, the Maharashtra State Road Development Corporation (MSRDC). In just nine years and 11 months.

The road transport system is under severe stress and the trans-oceanic bridge will be critical to facilitate more traffic and reduce pressure from the Mumbai-Pune Expressway, Mumbai-Chennai Highway and the Mumbai-Goa Highway and thus decongest the city.

This sea link will be the future of Mumbai Metropolitan Regions, which includes Navi Mumbai and will help gain quick access to the southern half of Navi Mumbai.

Maharashtra State Road Development Corporation Chairman and Public Works Minister, Anil Deshmukh says, "This is one of the biggest infrastructure projects in the country. Reliance will have to complete the project within five years, and will have to recover the cost within 10 years and hand over the project to us, the project will commence at the end of the year. It is a prestige issue and their name is at stake. I do not find that there are major challenges for Reliance to undertake the project and complete it within the stipulated time. We have taken clearances from the central government on environment, the archaeological survey of India and pollution control board." Meanwhile, Reliance Energy, Director, Reliance Energy J.P. Chalasani says, "We are completely prepared for the challenge. We have professionals and expert consultants to execute the sea link project in time."

The project, once executed is certain to revolutionise the real estate landscape of Navi Mumbai while opening up the hinterland for rapid development.

The Sewri-Nhava Sheva link is one of the vital components of a trinity of projects that are set to impact Navi Mumbai's real estate, experts point out–the other being the New International Airport likely to come up near Panvel and the massive SEZ being promoted by the Mukesh Ambani group.

It is these trinity of projects that will change Navi Mumbai from a distant suburb of Mumbai to a bustling mega-polis in its own right, real estate experts believe.

"So far Navi Mumbai's appeal has primarily been because of its relatively cheaper property rates and a better quality of life. This is resulted in several people moving to Navi Mumbai to stay while continuing to work in Mumbai. Thus, rather than becoming an alternate node of development, it has become another distant suburb of Mumbai," an analyst says.

While things have changed a bit in the last few years, with several companies setting up offices in Navi Mumbai, it is the Sewri-Nhava Sheva Sea Link along with the airport and SEZ that will make a crucial difference.

"Even within Navi Mumbai, development so far has been restricted to a few years like Vashi, Nerul, Belapur and Kharghar. The development potential of a vast hinterland still lies untapped. The Sewri Nhava Sheva Sea Link and related infrastructure development will uncork this potential" experts say.

(The above project case has been included here not exactly in the form of a Case Study material but for highlighting important issues in respect of on-coming mega infrastructure projects in India).

4. PROJECT FINANCE (LARGE & MEDIUM INDUSTRIAL UNITS) CASES FOR ANALYSIS & EVALUATION

CASE STUDY ON (A) JAI RUBBER TUBE PROJECT

M/s. Jai Bharat Rubber Tube Manufacturing Co. Ltd., newly incorporated company, decided to start the manufacturing of Rubber tube under NANO technology to be used by all types of vehicles. They have acquired land at GIDC, Fakirwala Town. They have submitted an application to grant a term loan for construction of factory building and purchase of plant and machinery. In response to their request they have submitted the following details:

- The Directors are from well-reputed group having experience of 10 years in the line of manufacturing of rubber tyres. Their flagship Company M/s. Bharat Tyre Manufacturing Co. Ltd. is dealing with Good Bank Ltd. since 1985. One of the directors is a technically well qualified having M.M. Rubber Technology from a reputed foreign university with specialization in Nano technology.

- The process knowhow for the proposed activities is to be supplied by an Indian organization *viz.*, Spectra Machine Tools Ltd. The suppliers have already supplied such plant to other leading tube manufacturing companies. The supplier has agreed to the terms and condition that 25% of the total cost will be released only after satisfactory trial run. As per the brochure submitted by Spectra Machine Tools Ltd., the minimum connected power load require is 125 KW for 100% capacity utilization.
- The Company has plans to market its production in bulk (50%) through tie up arrangement with leading vehicle manufacturing company. The rest 50% through their own retail showrooms. The brand name they want to create is "Jai Bharat". In bulk market the margin will be narrowed down but in retail sale the margin will be very high.

The cost and means of the project are as under:

Means of Financing	Rs. in Lac	Cost of Project	Rs. in Lac
Share capital fully paid up	4000	Cost of Land and Site dev.	390
Unsecured loans from friends and relatives of Directors	—	Cost of Construction	1500
Subsidy Receivable from State Government	1040	Cost of Machinery	6200
Term Loan	6400	Prov. for Contingency	750
		P & P Expenses	1350
		Margin on W.C.	850
		Misc Fixed assets	400
	11440		**11440**

The basic assumptions are:

1. The construction period will last for one year.
2. The Company would work for 300 days per year on two shift basis.
3. It is expected that the commercial production will start within 3 months from the completion of Construction of the project.
4. The company has estimated W.C. requirement of (figures in lac) Rs.2125, Rs.2530, Rs.2949, Rs.2951 and Rs.2953, at interest rate 12% p.a.
5. Estimated net profit after tax will be Rs.577, Rs.1127, Rs.1659, Rs.1706, Rs.1751 and Rs.1803.
6. They have estimated the selling price of Rs.12 per unit.

Details of Projections are as under:

	Year 1	Year 2	Year 3	Year 4	Year 5
Installed capacity (TPA)	2880	2880	2880	2880	2880
Term loan	6400	6000	5200	4400	3600
Working capital	2125	2530	2949	2951	2953
Capacity Utilisation (%)	50	60	70	70	70
Capacity Utilisation (AMT)	1440	1728	2016	2016	2016
Sales (Rs Th)	17280	20736	24192	24192	24192
Expenditure Raw material	11232	13478	15725	15725	15725
Power	691	829	968	968	968
Wages and salaries	900	1000	1200	1260	1323
Factory Overhead	50	53	56	60	64
Depreciation	696	696	696	696	696
Cost of production	13569	16057	18644	18708	18775
Gross profit	3711	4679	5548	5484	5417
Administrative expenses	100	100	100	100	100
Selling expenses	1728	2074	2419	2419	2419
Gross profit before intt	1883	2506	3028	2964	2897
Intt on T/L	896	896	812	700	588
Intt on W/C	383	455	531	531	532
Sub total	1279	1351	1343	1231	1120
Operating profit	604	1154	1686	1733	1778
Prel Exp written off	27	27	27	27	27
PBT	577	1127	1659	1706	1751
Provision for Tax	0	0	0	202	441
PAT	577	1127	1659	1505	1310
Cash accruals	1300	1850	2382	2228	2033
Dividend paid	—	480	480	560	640
Profit retained	577	647	1179	945	670
Net cash accrual	1300	1370	1902	1668	1393
1. Average DSCR 1.80					
2. Break even analysis BEP					
Units: 1186					
BEP Sales: 14235 (Th)					

TASK

- To analyse the cost of project and discuss each items of source of fund and its utilization.
- To undertake TEV study and Financial Viability.
- To draw conclusion for financing the project.

CASE STUDY ON (B) SOPHISTICATED WRIST WATCH PROJECT

- ABC Ltd is a new Public Ltd Company promoted by Mr. A and his sons Mr. B and Mr. C.
- They propose to set up a plant for manufacture of watch jewels with an installed capacity of 80 lac pcs per annum at Industrial estate, Jaipur, Rajasthan.
- Mr. A is mechanical engineer with MBA form a reputed Institution. His both the sons are engineers with MBA qualifications from USA. Mr. B has also worked at a reputed watch jewel manufacturer in Switzerland for about 7 years.
- Presently the family owns show rooms for reputed watches at various locations in Mumbai, Chennai and Delhi. They also undertake after sales service for watches and the repairs.
- Presently a major portion of the watch manufacturers is satisfied through imports. The all India consumption of watch jewels is estimated directly by contacting major manufacturers like M/s. HMT, M/s. Titan, etc. There is a clear demand supply gap of about 10.00 lac jewels per annum.
- Presently the cost of imported jewel (finished stage) is about Rs.45 for 100 pcs + customs duty of 75%. (Say Rs.80/- per 100 pcs). As against this the proposed sales price by M/s. ABC Ltd is Rs.65/- per 100 pcs.
- The main raw material required by the company is Ruby stone or sapphire stone. The Main suppliers are located at Rajasthan. They have shown willingness to enter into long term supply contract at the rate of Rs.1500 per kg. The requirement is estimated 1000 kg. per annum for production of 75 lac jewels **without wastage estimation.**
- The cost of 45 Nos. of semi skilled labourers is taken at Rs.1500 per month as per the prevalent laws.
- The applications for supply suitable infrastructure like power, water, effluent treatment etc. are made to the respective government authorities.

The Capital cost of project and means of finance thereof is as under:

Project cost	Rs. in Lac	Means of Finance	Rs. in Lac
Land	0.86	Share capital (incl. quasi equity of Rs.10.00 lac)	27.00
Building	4.50	Term Loan	30.00
Plant & Machinery			
Imported	28.00	State Govt. subsidy	9.85
Indigenous	4.00		
Customs @42% CIF	11.20		
Transportation/erection etc.	1.00		
Other fixed assets like quality assurance equipments etc.	2.20		
Premium and pre-op. expenses (includes interest of Rs.3.00 lac during construction period).	8.20		
Contingencies	5.90		
Margin for W.C.	0.99		
Total	**66.85**	**Total**	**66.85**

Task: To assess favourable and unfavourable points of the project based on the limited data/information as above with an assumption, however, that Co's Consultant has certified the viability of the Project.

❑❑❑

CHAPTER

10 Post-Disbursement Supervision

It is often said that the real job of a lending banker starts not with the sanction but on first disbursement of loans and advances as may have been sanctioned, in the form of Post-Disbursement Supervision (on site and off site) and that too, on a continuous basis and not continually. Post-disbursement supervision of infrastructure borrowal accounts may have an analogy with "After Sale Service" (of Machinery/Equipments' etc.) or post-operative care (surgical cases of patients) and as such, needs to be attended to with utmost care and attention so as to ensure safety of amounts lent to a borrower. The exposure in Infrastructure borrowal accounts is huge. Tangible security cover may often be a temporary comfort zone since recovery through such security sale is very difficult. Hence, a robust post-disbursement supervision mechanism is only, the real 'buffer' to the lender.

WHY POST-DISBURSEMENT SUPERVISION?

The important of post-disbursement supervision may be stated as under:

- This enables lending institution to exercise an on-site and off-site 'control' over the account.
- Physical Inspection of securities (charged to the lenders) as an on-site supervision process generally once in two months or earlier by lending officials, facilitates evaluation of condition and value of securities *vis-à-vis* amount lent end-use thereof and wherever necessary to initiate necessary protective measures as a proactive measure.
- Periodic verification of Books of Accounts, vouchers, invoices and other records maintained by the borrower as an off-site supervision process provides indication as to how the business affairs are being managed and to what extent amount lent remains safe in the hands of the borrower.
- Scrutiny of operations reflected in the account of the borrower provides clues as to the wellbeing or otherwise of the borrower and more specially to check up whether funds borrowed have been appropriately utilized.

- Interaction with the borrower/guarantor from time to time even informally may throw useful signals having a bearing on the account, *e.g.*, borrower's plan to reduce staff strength, selling out a portion of business land/building, etc. and accordingly the lender may exercise greater control.
- Verification of lending security documents from time to time at post-disbursement stages so as to ensure their validity and legal enforceability is possible only when effective post-disbursement supervision measure is initiated by the financing Bank.

In short, periodical inspection of securities, both moveable and immoveable as the case may be, verification of business records, etc. discussion with owners of the borrowing firm and on the top of all, examination of operation of Bank accounts are all the subject-matter of post-disbursement supervision, with the sole objective of ensuring safety of advance. Lending history of Commercial Banks/Financial institutions in India goes to show that ineffective/casual post-disbursement supervision often has failed to detect the weakness of borrowal account leading to lent-out funds in jeopardy.

On principle, there cannot be any stipulation as to the 'frequency' of such supervision. More frequent/continuous supervision ensures better prospects of safety of funds. Each Bank/Financial institutions has its own policy in the matter.

OVERALL GUIDELINES OF RESERVE BANK OF INDIA FOR ALL TYPES OF BORROWAL ACCOUNTS

It is the general requirement of RBI that financing Banks must have appropriate mechanism towards post-disbursement supervision of borrowal accounts, keeping in view the nature of accounts, size of credit limit, nature of securities charged to the Bank, etc. The frequency, modality, etc. are all left to each Bank, who must have documented guidelines to be followed by its official.

On 12.10.2002, RBI issued Guidelines Note on Credit Risk Management, wherein it is, *inter alia*, stated:

"Banks should establish proactive credit risk management practices like annual/half-yearly industry studies and individual obligor reviews, periodic credit calls that are documented, periodic visits of plant and business site and at least quarterly management reviews of troubled exposures/ weak credits."

From the angle of financing infrastructure Units, the following aspects of above guidelines of RBI have special bearing:

- Individual obligor reviews.
- Period credit calls/visits to plant and business site.

  Each Bank has generally a system of ANNUAL REVIEW of borrowal accounts focusing, *inter alia* on:

- Study of borrower's overall financial position yearwise (Balance Sheet) and business performances (P&L Account).
- Computation of Standard Accounting Ratios based on Balance Sheet and P&L Account and examination thereof from safety angle.
- How credit limits have been utilized over a period of 12 months generally-how was the experience of the Bank in handling the unit.
- How is the position of securities charged to the Bank with respect to condition, realizable value, etc.
- Market Report on the borrower and perception about the line of borrower's business.

If Bank is satisfied, credit limits may be continued or else exist strategies to be drawn in consultation with the borrower.

SOME CHECK POINTS

Keeping in view aforesaid overall guideline of RBI the following check points generally serve the purpose of an effective post disbursement supervision mechanism for infrastructure accounts.

(i) OFF-SITE

(*A*) For Term Loan and Deferred Payment Guarantee (DPG) Accounts:

— Whether for each disbursement adequate documentary evidence such as Invoice, CA's Certificate, Engineer's Certificate etc is on record.

— Whether interest due has been serviced in time.

— Whether 'Escrow Account' was maintained where stipulated–whether amounts are placed there regularly as may have been agreed to.

— In case some portion of sanctioned Term Loan limit has not been drawn within the agreed period, steps for cancellation be taken after ascertaining reasons for such non-drawal.

— In case of DPG Accounts whether any claim has been made on the bank by the beneficiary-if so why and how adjusted by the borrower.

— Whether insurance cover for the securities is in order.

(*B*) For Working Capital Accounts: Overdraft/Cash Credit

— Periodical verification of quantum of debit and credit operations in the accounts alongwith credits in 'Escrow Accounts' if any.

— Names of Parties in whose faster cheques are regularly issued and purpose of such payments.

— Whether there are frequent returns of cheques drawn on financial ground-if so reasons and remedial steps taken.

— Whether periodical statement of any hypothecated security, *e.g.*, spare parts considerable store etc is recovered on time.

— Whether insurance cover for the securities is in order.

ON-SITE SUPERVISION

This means physical inspection of securities as well as verification of business records mentioned by the borrower at the site, *e.g.*, documentary evidence of major receipts and payments and specially whether statutory payments all made in time.

On-site supervision may be done:

(*i*) Either, on surprise basis, *i.e.*, without prior intimation to the borrower.

(*ii*) Or, with prior intimation to the borrower.

While the conservative view is that surprise inspection is ideal, in reality inspection is undertaken generally with prior notice in order that the borrower remains free for interaction and also access to the site is possible without any constraint/formality. However, ideally once in a year or so attempts should be made for surprise inspection.

The fact however remains that on-site supervision must be extensive whether undertaken on surprise or with prior notice. During such inspection process following aspects need greater attention:

- Quality/condition and appropriate national realizable value of securities.
- If the project construction is in progress – details of work done and yet to be done with financial implications.
- If business has already commenced, Turnover as may be evidenced by record (*i.e.*, Sales/Maintenance).
- Accounting records for Inflows/Outflows.
- Verification of major items in Cash Book and General Ledger.
- Frequency of payments of statutory dues such as taxes, electricity bills and Provident Fund Contribution for Staff.
- Whether staff wages/salary paid on time.
- Human Relations (Staff) Management – whether there is any frequent distruption etc.

It may be stated in the context of off-site and on-site supervision that there is no standardized technique to be adopted by any lender. It is left to individual lender. However, if aforesaid aspects are taken care of, one may expect that supervision system would ensure safety of loan/advance.

MODALITY OF PHYSICAL INSPECTION OF SECURITIES/ OPERATION OF POWER PROJECT

1. Built stage and
2. Operations stage.

Following List is designed for a typical power project: The operators/ stake holders for a typical power project are:

1. SPV company-including private equity holders,
2. EPC Contractor,
3. O & M contractors,
4. SEBs–Purchaser/Power Wheeling arranger,
5. Fuel Supplier,
6. State Govt./GOI,
7. Lenders-Leader of Syndication.

The Inspection of a power project at Built Stage includes verification of contracts/documents-mainly from "Legal" perspectives as under:

1. **Power Purchase Agreement (PPA):** A typical power project includes generation facilities while for supply of the electricity generated; the transmission network owned by State Electricity Boards/Power Transmission Corporation etc is used. Under the circumstances, the parties to the PPA are the SPV and the SEB/ PTC etc. The normal clauses in the PPA contract include tariff or the selling price, selling arrangement, minimum guaranteed offtake, payment mechanism (during initial period-3-tier security mechanism was popular) etc.
2. **EPC Contract:** Engineering, Procurement and Construction contractor undertakes to hand over commissioned project from the stage of Engineering design, procurement of equipments and establishment to ensure successful operation as per the desired specifications. EPC contractors are primarily responsible for the plant's output as per the agreement–even if the project is partly sub-contracted.
3. **O&M Contract:** Operation & Maintenance of the plant & Equipments post successful commissioning by the EPC contractors is ensured by O&M contractors. In connection with physical assets, verification of documents may be undertaken as under:

Sr.No.	Type of Tangible Security	Documents required for verification	Remarks
1.	Project Land/ Building	**1.** NA certificate/Land Purchase Agreements. **2.** Title deed duly registered with the registrar of Assurances **3.** Building Plans approved by concerned of authority.	The ownership of the project land requires to be established so as to establish the owner. Buildings required for housing plant and machinery, utilities, offices, other support facilities requires to be ascertained. During visual inspection Buildings quick estimation of the constructed area be carried out for comparison with the approved plans.
2.	Plant and machinery	**1.** Original Bill of Purchase **2.** Copy of valuation Report by approved valuer (If purchased second hand) **3.** Audited Balance Sheet showing Fixed Assets schedules (Gross Block, Net Block, Depreciation etc. **4.** Valuer's Report **5.** Title deed duly registered with the registrar of Assurances	Visual Inspection of plant and machinery is required to ascertain the conditions of plant and machinery and its' wear and tear; if second hand. Any Major breakdown repairs done is available at the Log Book/records supplied by the original owner. Fast wearing parts like bearing sockets, Chains etc may be inspected for wear and tear etc.

2. **Operations Stage:** When a project has started commercial operations and the inspection is to be carried out subsequent to the announcement of start of commercial operations, following inspection formalities are useful:

Sr.No.	Type of Inventory	Documents required for verification	Remarks
1.	Raw Materials	**1.** Purchase Bills. **2.** Copy of L.R./R.R. of the material suppliers **3.** Excise Register (duly stamped by the excise authority)	Bills raised by Raw material suppliers are selected randomly for verification but at least one of latest date. In case the plant is Gas based and Fuel Supply Agreement (FSA) is executed, the same is to be verified for quality/quantity and unit rate of the fuel. Rates to be compared with published rates at technical journals/ Financial publications etc.

Sr.No.	Type of Inventory	Documents required for verification	Remarks
2.	Power sales realisation	Sales tax register. Copy of sales Invoices raised by the Company preferably client wise. Challans of advance CST/State ST paid.	1. Escrow Account operations are to be tallied with the Books of Accounts at the company. 2. The other operational cost details like employees cost, payment of infrastructure costs like water charges, O & M charges etc are to be tallied with the Books of Accounts at the company.

Notes

(*i*) The above modality is only an indicative one – it may be enlarged on case to case basis.

(*ii*) For other infrastructure projects the essence of above modality remains and each case is to be dealt with accordingly.

❑❑❑

CHAPTER 11 Accounting Standards and Audits

Evolution of Accounting Standards in world business management was propelled more by the disciplinary compulsion than out of internal necessities of industry, trade and commerce. It is a matter of fact that business transaction flows and events are not only required to be appropriately recorded on origin, but also that the outcome of transactional effects must be measured in terms of quantity, quality and value applied on a conservative and consistent basis period after period so long the business remains in operation.

Double Entry System of Accounting in vogue for about 300 years by now is the centre of gravity for development and implementation of accounting standards. In actual practice as double entry is generally the domain of corporates, by implication, accounting standards apply to limited companies, predominantly public limited companies in which category most of the infrastructure units are incorporated. The utility and efficacy of accounting standards is now widely established. However, depending on a country's social economic, business setting and laws in force, accounting standards may vary qualitatively as well as quantitatively except, of course, where International Accounting Standards and/or US GAAP (generally accepted accounting principles) are followed.

ACCOUNTING STANDARDS IN INDIA

The Institute of Chartered Accountants of India (1949 statute-born organization) acts as friend, philosopher and guide of private and public limited companies in regard to their classifying, recording and reporting of accounting transactions/events in order to achieve the objectives of conservatism, consistency transparency as well as disclosures of their operations for the sake of smooth flow of industry, trade and commerce. In Indian scenario predominant business role is performed by such organizations in value terms.

The Institute had set up its Accounting Standards Board in 1977 with a view mainly to achieve the following purposes:

- Need for creation of an uniform set of accounting principles for adoption by limited companies.

- Integration of age-old Indian accounting practices with International accounting standards over a period of time to the extent considered appropriate in Indian Business environment.
- Provision of an easy and convenient basis of comparison of financial position and business performances of various companies by the users of such information *viz.* Shareholders.
- Taxation Authorities, Regulatory Authorities and Creditors etc.
- Focussing on the 'watch-dog' function on the part of the members of the Institute (Chartered Accountants) thereby enabling them to form opinion annual/periodic financial statements of the companies strictly based on the applicable accounting standards. In the event of any deviation they have to report, the same clearly with the Management's explanations therefore.

TWENTY NINE INDIAN ACCOUNTING STANDARDS*

The Institute has already devised accounting standards applicable to the three levels of enterprises (Level 1, 2 & 3 details stated below).

Furthermore, as per the press report some accounting standards on derivative transactions are in the process of being evolved.

OVERALL CLASSIFICATION

Level 1: (A) Listed Companies

(B) Companies intending to go for listing

(C) Banks and Financial Institutions

(D) Insurance Companies

(E) Companies having business turnover (exclusive of other income) Over Rs. 50/- crore.

(F) Companies having borrowing (including public deposits) Over Rs. 10/- crore.

(G) Holding/Subsidiary companies of any of the above company.

Level 2: (A) Companies having business turnover (exclusive of other income) of over Rs. 40/- lac to Rs. 50/- crore

(B) Companies having borrowings (inclusive of Public Deposits) Over Rs.1/- crore but Upto Rs.10/- crore.

Level 3: Any company not falling under Level 1 or Level 2.

Infrastructure Companies may generally fall under Level 1.

---

* Since reduced to 28-.

Issues covered under the existing accounting standards are summarised below:

(Most of the standards may generally apply to Infrastructure Companies)

Accounting Standard No.	Issues covered	Type of Enterprise** (Level 1-3) to comply
AS:1	Disclosure of accounting policies	All the three enterprises *i.e.*, level 1, 2, & 3
AS:2	Valuation of Inventories	All the three enterprises-however not applicable progress in construction contracts, producer invention such as live stock, agricultural and forest products, oils, ores and gases. Also banking and insurance company not fall under this category.
AS:3	Cash Flow Statements	Level 1 Enterprises
AS:4	Contingencies and events after Balance Sheet date	All the three enterprises except life and general insurance companies
AS:5	Net Profit/Loss for the period, prior period items and changes in accounting policies	
AS:6	Depreciation Accounting	All the three enterprises in respect of their depreciation except forest plantations, wasting assets, minerals, plantations, goodwill and live stock
AS:7	Construction Accounting Contracts	Enterprises (all levels) undertaking construction business
AS:8**	Accounting for research and development	All the three enterprises
AS:9	Revenue Recognition	All the three enterprises
AS:10	Accounting for fixed assets	All the three enterprises
AS:11	The effects of changes in foreign exchange rates	All the three enterprises
AS:12	Accounting for Govt. grants	All the three enterprises but does not seem to apply Banking companies
AS:13	Accounting for investment	All the three enterprises–especially relevant for banking companies
AS:14	Accounting for amalgamations	All the three enterprises
AS:15	Accounting for retirement benefits in the financial statements of employers	All the three enterprises
AS:16	Borrowing costs	All the three enterprises
AS:17	Segment reporting	Level 1 enterprises
AS:18	Related party disclosures	Level 1 enterprises

Accounting Standard No.	Issues covered	Type of Enterprise** (Level 1-3) to comply
AS:19	Lease	All the three enterprises except for leases for exploration of natural resources, licensing agreements for motion films and lease for land
AS:20	Earning per share	All the three enterprises
AS:21	Consolidated financial statement	All the three enterprises
AS:22	Accounting for taxes on income	All the three enterprises
AS:23	Accounting for investments in associates in consolidated financial statements	All the three enterprises
AS:24	Discontinuing Operations	All the three enterprises
AS:25	Interim Financial Reporting	Not mandatory
AS:26	Intangible assets	Level 1 enterprises
AS:27	Financial reporting of interest in Joint Venture	All the three enterprises
AS:28	Impairment of assets	All the three enterprises
AS:29*	Provisions, contingent liabilities and contingent assets	All the three enterprises

** Since withdrawn.

* Now reduced to 28- Standards.

COMPLIANCE ISSUES: INFRASTRUCTURE PROJECTS

Infrastructural Development Companies/Special Purpose Vehicles for infrastructure projects in India are all Corporate entities – Private Limited or Public Limited Companies. Hence, as per regulatory requirements they are required to comply with aforesaid Accounting Standards as may be applicable to them while finalizing Accounts as also reporting thereof to various authorities. A lending bank/financial institutions has, as such no direct role to play in the connection.

However, indirectly they have to ensure the above compliance by the infrastructure project borrowers. This is done by insisting that an application for credit facility cannot be considered further if the borrowers does not follow laid down accounting standards and the statutory Auditor makes a references to that effect and issues 'Qualified Report'.

STATUTORY/CONCURRENT AUDIT

Infrastructure projects are undertaken in India generally under Corporate form of organization even when Public Private Partnership (PPP) model is adopted. Hence, as per prevailing statutory framework such organizations have to arrange their accounts audited atleast annually by a qualified Chartered Accountant. The auditing framework (under the supervision of Institute of Chartered Accountants of India) being very extensive, provides a comfort to the lenders in regard to safety of their funds. For obvious reasons, in case of any serious qualifying remark is made by the auditor, the lenders may tighten their belt to protect their loans in an appropriate manner.

Besides annual/periodic statutory audit, it also advisable that in case of large financial comments to any infrastructure organisation, an arrangement may be required by way of Concurrent Audit. This may be broadly be as under:

- Concurrent Auditor need not necessarily be a Chartered Accountant. But such an auditor must be well versed in financial accounts and finance matters.
- Concurrent Auditor should verify on an ongoing basis inflow and outflow of funds and draw his opinion.
- Expenses for Concurrent Auditor to be borne by the company although selection of such auditor will be the prerogative of the lenders.
- Coconut Auditor should directly report to the lenders at least on a monthly basis – in serious matters instant reporting is required.

The main benefit for the lenders in such an arrangement is that in appropriate cases the lender may immediately take up with the borrowers for rectifying the issues to their satisfaction for the eventual protection of the loans and advances.

❑❑❑

CHAPTER

12 Risk Management Implications

It has already been accepted as universal financial prudence that any grant of fund-based facilities (Loan, O/D, etc.) or non-funded facilities (Guarantee, Letters of Credits etc.) by a lender must be backed by an appropriate capital adequacy (internationally 8% but RBI has prescribed 1% higher, *i.e.*, 9%). This is primarily to ensure that any default by the lender is, to a certain extent covered by the lender's own stake as a part of credit risk management in banking system.

Hitherto, as per Basel Accord-I prescriptions, exposures of any kind used to attract 100% Risk Weight. However, Basel Accord-II, under implementation in India, in commercial banking system seeks to implant an element of flexibility in the operation of capital adequacy requirements so that on an international level competition amongst the Banks is not handicapped owing to capital adequacy requirements "One size fits for all" approach as is under Basel Accord-I, has very rightly been given go by in the interest of healthy growth of Commercial Banks Operating in India under Basel II. Financial exposure in Infrastructure sector is huge – unit-wise. Hence, risk management implications deserve special treatment.

INFRASTRUCTURE RISK SEGMENTATION

Infrastructure sector, through containing significant societal overtone and is mostly sovereign activated and patronized, involves a variety of business risks. As a result, the wellbeing of the project may suffer with a telling effect on repayment obligations of financial obligations if adequate risk mitigating system is not put in place.

No business risk can truly be segmented, the effect of one risk may cast a shadow directly or indirectly on other risk. Infrastructure project as a broad-based category (without in-category classifications like, power, telecom, Road etc.), main items of risk as under need special attention:

1. **Construction Risk:** This arises when certain unexpected developments (*e.g.*, social unrest/political issues for land acquisition for expressway etc.) occur during the construction period of the project which may cause
   (*a*) delay in execution/completion of the project
   (*b*) Cost over runs
   (*c*) Shortfalls in performance parameters.

   The intensity of construction risk is more in large capital intensive and long construction period projects such as power, road etc., while considerably low in sectors like telecommunications, *e.g.* In order to mitigate the risk the sponsors of the project (*i.e.*, owners/Operators) may shift a portion of risk to the Project Contractors who agree to provide turnkey projects with provision for imposition of penalty in case of their failure.
2. **Operation Risk:** This arises when technical performance of the Project (*e.g.*, power generation per day etc.) falls below the original projection. Such a risk is more pronounced in case of project based on untried/fast changing technology such as telecommunications while very low in case of power plans and roads etc.

   As a safeguard measure the sponsors may entrust the matter to experienced Operators and Maintenance Contractors with built-in provison in the Contract for claim of liquidated damages in case of any shortfall in performance.
3. **Revenue Collection Risk:** Non-receipt of payment for services such as power bill, toll cess creates such a risk. This is more in case buyers of services are one/very few like State Electricity Boards for power supply etc.

   To avoid/reduce the above risk the sponsors may seek Government Guarantee or any other avenues on case to case basis.
4. **Regulatory Risk:** An infrastructure project is dependent upon the regulatory framework of the country where it operates throughout the life of the project. Regulations/Rules are again linked with the Complextion/Priority of the Government from time. Tariff formula for services may be changed/modified when considered necessary either with the power of the provisions in the contract or by Governmental directive etc.

   The effects of such risks are relatively less if there is a separate and independent regulatory authority, *e.g.*, Telecom Regulatory Authority etc.

5. **Political Risk:** Infrastructure Projects are used by the masses and, as such, have "high visibility and strong public interest". Arising out of this, political act may interrupt or upset the commercial terms or even complete cancellations of the project.

In the Indian context, there is hardly any risk mitigant in this respect. However, wherever scope of any Multilateral Investment Guarantee or Bilateral Investment Protection Agreements exists, political risk may partially be covered up.

BASEL-II RISK MANAGEMENT IMPLICATIONS

Basel Accord II (of Bank for International Settlements, Switzerland) is applicable for infrastructure lending (like any other form of lending) by Commercial Banks. The Accord (to which India is a party) is aimed at ensuring a robust banking system by putting in place a full package of safeguards for three risk classes of banks *viz.* Credit Risk, Market Risk and Operational Risk. For Infrastructure exposure, credit risk is the main issue for banks.

The guideline as applicable for infrastructure provides for Three Pillars:

Pillar I	:	Minimum Capital Requirements (for any funded and Non-funded exposure by any bank).
Pillar II	:	Supervisory Review Process (Role and responsibility of RBI as regards implementations of risk management Process mainly in respect of lendings by banks).
Pillar III	:	Market Discipline (the periodical disclosures to the Members of the public by banks about their lendings and other matters).

In respect of Pillar I, the applicable risk weight is as per external credit ratings or by a bank's internal credit ratings (in India, for the present, banks will go by credit rating of approved Credit Rating Agencies). The Credit rating process may be involved generally for application of risk weight between 20% and 150% for funded credit exposure. In addition, for non-funded exposure (*e.g.*, Letter of Credit/Guarantee) risk weight there is provision of maximum 100% risk weight). Since Pillar I is for computation of minimum Capital requirement this aspect may be viewed from following example:

(*i*) *Term Loan of Rs. 100 crore from:* To Bhagawan Bharasha Expressway Ltd by Good Bank Ltd.

(*ii*) *Deferred Payment Guarantee/Stand by L/C Rs.100 crore:* To Bhagawan Bharasha Expressway Ltd from the same Bank.

Computation of total Credit exposure as account of the borrower

Funded	:	Rs. 100 crore
Non-funded	:	Rs. 100 crore
Total	:	Rs. 200 crore

Assuming that the account is excellent and approved external credit rating agency proposes 20% risk weight, the minimum capital which Good Bank will be required to hold for the account is:

20% of Rs.200 crore = Rs.40 crore

∴ Minimum Capital requirements in India 9% (minimum 8% as per Accord but by RBI has prescribed 1% additional)	Rs.3.60 crore (9% of Rs.40 crore)

Pillar II being the responsibility of RBI, they will evaluate through periodical off-site and on-site verification of the records of Good Bank whether appropriate capital holding is there in the bank for all its exposure and, also in general, bank's risk management architecture and system and practices. They may, where considered necessary, ask bank even to maintain more than prescribed 9% capital.

Pillar III provides for the periodical disclosure about all credit exposures (including infrastructure exposure) – qualitative as well as qualitative aspects. Any omission of material disclosure may prompt RBI to initiate corrective action against any bank.

In short, therefore, there is no specific implication for infrastructure exposure by any bank – all the guidelines of the Accord as applicable for other sectors will arise for infrastructure sector as well. Only point is that as financial volume of infrastructure sector is comparatively large, capital buffer and risk management implications have to be different and more focused.

ASSET-LIABILITY MISMATCH

From the angle of Banks/Financial Institutions, funds provided to any infrastructure borrower may take any/both of the following:

- Term Loan
- Subscription to their Long term Bonds/Securities of under the category : Investment.

In both the above situations the item/items will be on the Asset side of Bank/Financial Institution.

Since term Loans are usually of a very long period of say 15 years + and similarly are their Bonds/Securities, the lenders also need their long term resources which are possible generally through following:

- Raising their Capital funds.
- Mobilising other means of resources such as Perpetual Debt Instruments, Perpetual Non-Cumulative Preference Share, Hybrid Debt Capital Instruments. Besides the above, it may also be possible, in some cases, to take recourse to Take-out route and Refinance from Refinancing Institutions such as Infrastructure Finance Development Co. as stated in earlier Chapter on "Finance for Infrastructure".

If adequate long-term resources are built-up in the manner outlined above, then obviously there would not any case of asset-liability mismatch. In this context, RBI guideline states as under:

"The long-term financing of infrastructure projects may lead to asset-liability mismatches, particularly when such financing is not in conformity with the maturity profile of a bank's liabilities. Banks would, therefore, need to exercise due vigil on their asset-liability position to ensure that they do not run into liquidity mismatches on account of lending to such project".

DISCLOSURE OF EXPOSURE TO INFRASTRUCTURE SECTOR

Under Pillar No.3 (Market Discipline) obligation of Basel Accord II, banks extending credit to infrastructure sector, have, interalia to disclose periodically (thru' Audited Annual Report and Bank's Website) amount of exposure-fund-based and non-fund based and in case any such exposure is classified or non-performing, bifurcation in the form of substandard and Doubtful Components is to be indicated. The basic objective of such a disclosure mechanism is to enable members of the public to assess the operation of banks on an ongoing basis.

It may, incidentally, be stated that banks are, however, no obligation to disclose this details of infrastructure borrowal such as Names, Amount lent, Terms and Conditions etc. as these are of confidential nature between bank and borrower.

IS THERE ANY SPECIAL INCENTIVE FOR LENDING TO INFRASTRUCTURE SECTOR FROM BASEL II ANGLE?

In order to assess incentive aspect in respect of infrastructure lending the following aspects need to be looked into:

- Infrastructure lending is generally more credit risk-prone as realization if any defaulted credit through the sale of tangible securities is an extremely difficult and complicated process.

- But, in some cases for such exposures Government Guarantee is available which technically provides 100% comfort to any lending bank.
- Infrastructure lending, though is of long duration one (generally over 15 year tenor), there is a scope of Take-out as per RBI guideline after a couple of years if a lending bank/financial institutions chooses to unload its exposure.
- National Priority lies on infrastructure financing – hence for Public Sector banks/Financial Institutions, it is more an obligation and not of choice really to lend subject however, to project being found techno economic viability – of course non-viable projects are not to be entertained at all.
- Infrastructure lending is extended on commercial terms, hence banks/financial institutions earn reasonable rate of return on such exposures in the form of interest, service charges, fees etc.

  In the context aforesaid, each credit application from an infrastructure unit is required to be evaluated by the concerned bank from cost-benefit angle keeping in view however, national priority aspects and the quality of the project.

SHOULD THERE BE ANY CREDIT GUARANTEE ORGANISATION AS AN EFFECTIVE RISK MITIGANT?

For export credit, guarantee cover from Export Credit Guarantee Corporation (ECGC) is available. Again for loans/advances to Small Scale Industries/SME sector, Credit Guarantee Fund Trust provides protection to a lending banker. But Infrastructure sector does not fit in any such external Credit Guarantee mechanism.

With a view to providing significant incentives to lending by banks/financial institutions and in the context of boosting up infrastructure developments all around, the Authorities may like to promote in near future a public sector infrastructure Credit Guarantee Organisation providing for at least 50% guarantee protection on recovering guarantee commission of say 1% p.a.

❑❑❑

CHAPTER

13 Recovery of Non-Performing Accounts**

Non-Performing Advances (NPA), which is termed as Non-Performing Loans (NPA) in many countries, is generally the outcome of ineffective/faulty Credit Risk Management in an Institution. More often than out, problems are not recognized at early stages and hence, remedial actions are not initiated in time. This is precisely the reason for RBI advising Banks (on Credit Risk Guidance Note issued on 12.10.2002), *inter-alia*, as under:

"Banks should have a consistent approach towards early problem recognition, the classification of problem exposures and remedial action."

The aforesaid regulatory advice is applicable for all types of borrowal accounts including infrastructure accounts.

NPA DEFINED

There was no statutory definition of NPA in India till the promulgation of The Securitisation and Reconstruction of Financial Assets and Enforcement of Security Interest Act, 2002. Now, Section 2(O) of the Act defines as under:

"Non-Performing Asset" means an asset or account of a borrower which has been classified by a Bank or Financial Institution as sub-standard, doubtful or loss asset in accordance with the directions or guidelines relating to asset classification issued by the Reserve Bank of India."

In other countries, Central Banking Regulatory Authorities issue directives taking into their local conditions as to the circumstances/situation when a credit exposure (including Investment) is to be treated as non-performing impaired/delinquent/in default.

Reserve Bank of India has directed that if in respect of an exposure payment of interest/repayment of instalment of principal or both remaining

** Some portion of this Chapter has been drawn from Author's book on *Credit Risk Management*.

unpaid for a period of 90 days, such exposure is to be treated as Non-performing.

The basic ingredient of NPA is Default in respect of interest when due and instalment when due as per the contract terms.

No standardized definition of Wilful Default has so far been evolved. In essence, Wilful Default may be defined as any non-payment of commitment by an obligor with the sole intent of causing financial harm to any lender even when the inability is not caused by cash crunch or asset crunch. Situation of Wilful Default is generally the consequence of siphoning off funds by means of fraud/misappropriation.

Cases of wilful default need stern action – including filing of criminal suit when so advised.

QUICK MORTALITY

Internal reasons and external reasons (except the case of Wilful Default), leading to an account being NPA do not erupt usually in the short run and may even take 2-3 years for a perceptible bearing on the fulfillment of financial obligations by a borrower. In the interim, of course, warning signals may flow in to the lender in doses. However, there may be situations when soon after disbursement, the account shows full symptoms of NPA. Quick Mortality of an exposure (account) occurs if signs/symptoms of full-scale default are noticed generally within a period of 12-18 months, forcing lenders to crystallize the securities and/or to initiate appropriate recovery steps.

Following are the main causes of Quick Mortality cases:

- Siphoning off funds through fraud/misappropriation (wilful default) by the borrower.
- Sudden appearance of a cheaper close substitute product (this may, however, be considered as a factor of inefficient management) which, however, for all practical purposes does not arise in case of infrastructure sector.

Quick Mortality is generally the outcome of Wilful Default.

DIVERSION OF FUNDS BY ANY SME – WHO IS TO BE BLAMED?

Diversion of funds availed for a particular purpose/project to unauthorized purpose/project may turn an account into NPA. The moot question remaining here is who is to be blamed for the situation happening – is it that the borrower is solely responsible or is it that the contributory negligence of Bank/Financial Institution is the reason, cannot be always ruled out. It is thus, difficult to conclude in a definitive manner. However, following aspects are to be considered:

- Borrowers are expected to utilize the funds for the purposes for which they are availed. Thus, they are prima facie to be blamed/ accountable for any diversion.
- Banks/Financial Institutions also have to exercise due diligence to ensure end-use of funds. Credit Risk Architecture & Management should be well articulated not only to detect at a later stage any diversion but to prevent any attempt by any borrower to divert funds for unauthorised purposes. Post-disbursement supervision and follow up should be effective. Mere obtaining of appropriate covenants in security documents signed by the borrower may not be of good use unless appropriate system is in place.

ACTION FLOW CHART IN NPA RECOVERY IN CASE OF INFRASTRUCTURE ADVANCES

- To identify NPA with the tool of Credit Rating (a considerable downgrade in a short period is a direct indication) and/or other tools, (*e.g.*, depletion of security cover/operation in accounts) as to accounts which can be turned viable over a time horizon with a planned Rehabilitation/Nursing programme.
- Unviable accounts where EXIT strategies by way of:
  (*i*) Crystallization/Sales of assets.
  (*ii*) For the deficit, if any, to decide Compromised Settlement with/without any sacrifice or to initiate legal action by filing of suit.
- For both viable and non-viable appropriate provisioning as per regulatory guidelines should be made/held during the subsistence of the account.

  (In some countries, at the commencement of disbursement of any credit some provisions are made and are progressively increased as a 'buffer'. In India, as per RBI guidelines, even for accounts classified as Standard Assets, notional provision is to be made).
- Corporate Debt Restructuring (for accounts with exposure of Rs.20 crore and above under consortium/syndicate/multiple banking arrangement) is to be initiated as per regulatory guidelines, considering that eligible accounts are viable in the long run most of the infrastructure borrowal accounts may fall under this category).

RECOVERY WINDOW THROUGH SARFAESI ACT, 2002 – EFFECTIVENESS IN CASE OF INFRASTRUCTURE ACCOUNTS

The Securitisation and Reconstruction of Financial Asset and Enforcement of Security Interests Act (SARFAESI) 2002 has put in place as comprehensive platform for prompt and effective recovery of NPAs of banks/financial institutions especially in cases of large exposures. The salient features of this law as applicable to infrastructure accounts are as under:

- Assets of borrower/guarantor as are legally charged in favour of the lender qualify for this specific recovery window subject to the outstanding exposure being over Rs.1 Lac and also on compliance of other relevant provisions of SARFAESI ACT.
- Upon serving demand notice with permissible time-bond and in the event of non-payment within the notice period, bank/financial institutions extending secured advances such as Hypothecation/ Mortgage of movable/immovable assets of any – borrower including infrastructure accounts, may seek assistance from Chief Metropolitan Magistrate or District Magistrate for taking physical provision of the charged securities.
- Debt Recovery Tribunal is only empowered to decide on any objection of the borrower/guarantor about the lender's right to take physical passion of securities. No civil court has jurisdiction to entertain any such objection even in circumstances where there is suit/proceeding existing.
- The Act provides protection to the lenders/their officers for any action initiated for recovery of defaulted advance provided the some has been done in good faith.
- When a guarantor mortgages his/her personal property (as an additional cushion for the lender), the lender cannot, however, take benefit of provisions of SARFAESI Act. In such cases usual legal procedure is to be followed.

It is apparent from the above that SARFAESI Act provides an effective recovery window in respect of defaulted infrastructure accounts in view of the following:

(*i*) Speedy and clear mechanism for taking physical possession of securities by the lender.

(*ii*) Assistance from Chief Metropolitan Magistrate District Magistrate would be available for a secured creditor taking physical possession.

(*iii*) Borrower/Guarantor interfering lawful rights of taking physical possession of securities by approaching Civil Court is not possible since such courts do not have jurisdiction to try such cases.

(*iv*) Legal Cost of recovery incurred by lender is substantially reduced since SARFAESI Act provides appropriate and speedy mechanism to address concerns of secured creditors.

(v) Infrastructure borrowal accounts of banks/financial institutions are generally on secured basis (except in rare cases of allowing temporary overdraft without any tangible security cover) and are over the cut off limit of Rs.1 Lac. Hence the provisions of the Act are beneficial to such lenders.

STAFF ACCOUNTABILITY

Staff Accountability means the process of exploring the reasons for any action/inaction on the part of a Functionary relating to a particular subject/situation/matter. Accountability improves decision-making.

Professional Management in an organisation demands professional decision-making, that is to say, for any action/inaction, there must be an unambiguous and clear 'reasons' – 'transparency' being an essential ingredient.

In credit matters, the decision-making by a Functionary involves multi-dimensional situations beginning with receipt of Application for credit culminating in 'Sanction' or 'Rejection'. When sanctioned, the entire gamut of Post-disbursement Supervision and Follow up has to be carried out so as to ensure at any point of time "asset quality".

Hence, in the entire roadmap, there may be cases when a Functionary could be negligent and/or dishonest in performing his role. Therefore, when a credit account (or for that matter in any decision-output) turns 'sour', staff accountability is required to be undertaken with a Three-Fold purpose:

- Correcting/Rectifying official/s responsible for any action/inaction and in extreme circumstances, getting rid of such officials from the organisation.
- To lay greater emphasis from action point on *mala fide* act as distinguished from *bona fide* acts.
- Where necessary to reorient organisational rules/procedures/systems so as to be more focused on compliance.

In Indian Banking/Financial System, Staff Accountability studies are originated generally when an asset quality slips from 'Standard' category (also known as 'Pass' category in some countries) with the following main purposes:

- Officials responsible are 'identified'.
- Measurement of damage in asset quality is made linking it to lapses on the part of the identified officials.
- Appropriate action (which may even include 'reskilling' the officials whose lapses were unintentional/innocent ones) against identified officials are promptly taken.
- The process may act as a deterrent measure for other officials against any violation of norms/rules/guidelines.

MAIN POINTS IN STAFF ACCOUNTABILITY STUDIES ON CREDIT QUALITY SLIPPAGE

Staff Accountability studies should be carried out on "Watch-dog" approach and NOT on "Blood-hound" approach. In order that such studies in respect of Credit failures are undertaken in a professional manner and free from 'bias', the following main points should feature in such studies in a Bank/Financial Institution:

- Whether Credit Proposal was appraised in accordance with laid down norms and guidelines, including credential investigation of proposed borrower/guarantor.
- Whether Pre-sanction site visit/asset inspection was carried out and was found in order.
- Whether terms and conditions, securities and covenants were stipulated as per laid down norms/guidelines.
- Whether security documentation was in order and where necessary, specific vetting of Legal Official was obtained.
- Whether first disbursement of credit was made after complete and perfect documentation and on compliance of all the stipulated terms and conditions of sanction.
- Whether Post-disbursement Supervision and Follow-up was undertaken as per laid down norms and guidelines.
- Whether all 'material' events noticed in any credit exposure were brought to the notice of appropriate authorities including communication to Reserve Bank of India, if necessary.
- Whether any 'malafide' action/inaction on the part of any official was noticed.
- Views of the Investigating Officer as to the reasons for slippage in asset quality in an exposure.

Since infrastructure advances accounts are generally sanctioned, monitored and controlled by a number of secured creditors together (under consortium/syndication form of lending), barring exceptional circumstances the impact of any staff accountability study for such accounts would be quite limited.

❑❑❑

ANNEXURE

MODEL APPLICATION FORM for FINANCIAL ASSISTANCE for INFRASTRUCTURE SECTOR and OTHER SECTORS

Date of Application: **Annexure**

S.No.	Particulars	Detail
1.	Name of Applicant Firm/Company:	
2.	Constitution	
3.	Date of Establishment/Date of Incorporation (2-copies of Memorandum and Articles of Association to be sent along with this application in case of Private/Public LTD Companies)	
4.	Nature of business activity already being undertaken/proposed to be undertaken.	
5.	Date of Commencement of existing business activity (if any)/tentative date of Commencement of proposed business activity.	
5A.	2-copies of latest Audited Balance Sheets – if applicable:	
6.	Full Address of Head office/Registered office/ Principal place of business-existing/proposed.	
6A.	Location of existing project area / proposed project area.	
7.	Names of owners (in case of Proprietary/ Partnership Concerns)/Directors (in case of Private/Public LTD Companies and their detailed professional/business background (this to be furnished in a separate sheet along with this application.	
8.	% Share holding of Directors.	
9.	Full Names and Residential Addresses of Proprietor/Partners/Directors.	
10.	Business/Industrialist Group to which the firm/ Co. belongs to – if applicable.	
11.	Present Banking Arrangement, if any, in the name of the Applicant – if applicable and also banking arrangement of main promoters.	
12.	Gist of activity proposed to be taken up for which financial assistance required.	
13.	Gist of Financial Highlights in the following manner for the business – separate for existing business, if any, and proposed business: A. Cost of Project and Means of Finance. B. Gist Projected Balance Sheet, Profit/ Loss Account and Cash Flows for the firm/ organization as a whole and separate for the Project for which financial assistance is required.	To be submitted in separate sheets

S.No.	Particulars	Detail
14.	In case of an existing business whether at any time Credit Rating from an approved Credit Rating agency was obtained – if so, details thereof.	
15.	Details of Financial Assistance required:	

Nature of Financial assistance	Quantum (i.e. Limit)	From which banks/ financial institution expected	proposed repayment terms	Securities to be offered	Interest rate expected from banks Financial institution

16.	Whether Techno-Economic Viability Report from an approved organization obtained – if so 2-copies of Report to be sent along with this application 1.	
17.	Gist of SWOT Analysis (Strength, Weakness, Opportunities & Threat) of the proposed activity.	

UNDERTAKING

This Application for credit facility/ies is being submitted by us in full knowledge and understanding that there is no commitment from the bank/s/Financial Institutions to consider the credit facilities in full/or in part as applied for. The application may be examined entirely at the sole discretion of bank/s Financial Institutions and we undertake not to raise any issue in this respect at all.

Signature:

Proprietor / Partners / Directors / with SEAL

❑❑❑